PAPER
Transformed

QUARRY

PAPER Transformed

A Handbook of Surface-Design Recipes and Creative Paper Projects

BEVERLY MASSACHUSETTS

QUARRY BOOKS

Julia Andrus

First published in the United States of America by
Quarry Books, a member of
Quayside Publishing Group
100 Cummings Center
Suite 406-L
Beverly, Massachusetts 01915-6101
Telephone: (978) 282-9590
Fax: (978) 283-2742
www.quarrybooks.com

Library of Congress Cataloging-in-Publication Data

Andrus, Julia.
   Paper transformed: a handbook of surface-design recipes and creative paper projects/
Julia Andrus.
     p. cm.
  ISBN 1-59253-370-1 (pbk.)
  1. Paperwork—Handbooks, manuals, etc. 2. Art—Technique—Handbooks, manuals,
etc. I. Title.
TT870.A476 2007
745.54—dc22

                             2007001047
                             CIP

ISBN-13: 978-1-59253-370-1
ISBN-10: 1-59253-370-1

10 9 8 7 6 5 4 3 2 1

Design: Judy Morgan
Cover design: Rockport Publishers
Cover Image: Glenn Scott Photography
Photography: Glenn Scott Photography and Julia Andrus Design Studio

Printed in Singapore

CONTENTS

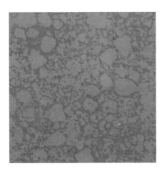

CHAPTER ONE

Old Favorites and New Variations

CHAPTER TWO

Original Designer Papers

CHAPTER THREE

Metal Look-Alikes

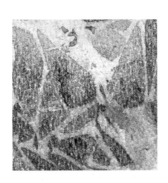

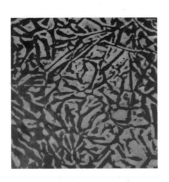

Introduction

I HAVE HAD THE RARE OPPORTUNITY TO share and teach art processes in many parts of the world. I recently taught a workshop in France and did my best to deliver a great part of my presentation in the native language of those I was teaching. When I was finished, I looked around the room and was touched by the tables strewn with art supplies and mediums and by the beautiful projects each participant had created. I apologized for any difficulty they may have had in understanding me, but I said at least we had a universal language between us—the language of art. If there were barriers between us they melted away in an instant as they stood up and applauded my sentiments. The workshop ended with many embraces, kisses, and nods. We understood each other perfectly.

Such is the power of art. It is about relationships. What begins as an act of self-expression becomes a revealing connection when shared with others. Art truly is a universal language and there are countless methods and mediums through which we can communicate. However, of all the mediums available throughout the world, none is more widely used or more readily available than paper.

Paper is everywhere. Paper in and of itself can be art, yet in its simplest form it begs for transformation, to be written and drawn on, painted, folded, cut, molded, and altered. This book is about transforming paper and using paper as the foundation for creative expression. Included are many traditional processes as well as a host of new and original techniques. It is meant to inspire and serve as a resource during the design process.

Therefore, I would like to extend this invitation to all artists, crafters, designers, and would-be artists: The next time you are looking for a creative outlet, put it on paper, that most universal of all mediums. Paint it, wrinkle it, stamp on it, emboss it, fold it, rip it, and write on it. And when you're done, share your art with someone else.

Happy creating!

—*Julia*

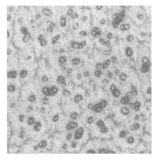   

 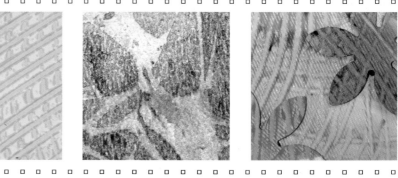 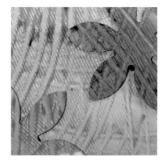

 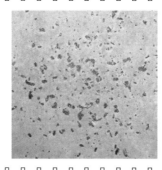

CHAPTER ONE

Old Favorites and New Variations

Before paper was invented, mankind was drawn to visual expression using an assortment of materials, pigments, and dyes. Imagine an individual taking a berry and scraping it against a rock to leave a trail of color and texture. Many of the processes included in this chapter have been used for centuries. They are the foundation for transforming paper and continue to inspire new generations of artists who add to the traditional methods with new renditions and applications. This chapter includes many traditional tried-and-true recipes as well as a host of imaginative variations.

ABOUT MARBLING

Creating the look of marble on paper is an ancient art that has challenged and intrigued artists for centuries. Marbling techniques have evolved through the ages and have become a highly accomplished art form. Marbled papers have been used to cover walls, adorn books and objects, embellish manuscripts, and delight the eye with their singular beauty.

There have been volumes written about marbling techniques, mediums, and methods. Marbling is basically a process by which paints are floated and swirled on a water bath. When the paper is laid into the bath, designs are created wherever the paint is deposited. Variations in design are created by "raking" the paints with wires, brushes, or a variety of tools to create intricate patterns.

There are basically two types of marbling techniques and a number of variations built upon these basic techniques. The first uses a base, or *size*, which thickens the water and allows the paints to float on top. The paper is treated with a *mordant*, which conditions it to absorb the paint better. This is the type of marbling used to create more intricate patterns. This is done by manipulating the paint into designs and patterns before laying the paper down.

The other marbling technique requires only paint and water. Using water with watercolors, pastels, or other dry pigments is a method that has been used for centuries by Asian artisans, and although it is more difficult to control the effects of the design than in the previous method, the spontaneous effects are just as intricate and equally amazing. This method can also be done with oil colors that have been thinned with turpentine.

Marbling base, or *size*, is made of chemicals that thicken the water and allow the paints to float on the surface. The two most commonly used sizes are methylcellulose and carrageenan (a natural seaweed product). However, there are other methods that use a variety of creative substances for sizing. These include gum tragacanth, gelatin, liquid or powdered starches, and wallpaper pastes. Even thick hair conditioner or shaving cream can work. Imagination rules when it comes to choosing a size, and experimentation is part of the process—it's part of the allure of marbling!

A mordant is used to pretreat paper and helps it absorb pigments better. Two tablespoons (about 30 g) of alum dissolved into two cups (about ½ L) of hot water makes an excellent paper mordant. The solution should be

TIPS

- For small-batch marbling, a glass baking dish makes a good tray and cleans up easily.
- To learn to marble or for quick and easy applications, there are excellent kits available from art supply outlets.

allowed to air-dry on the paper so it conditions properly.

The term *dispersing* refers to how the paints respond when they come in contact with the water or size solution. Every pigment will respond differently because it has its own unique chemistry. Some pigments spread more, some need thinning, some are heavier, some change color when diluted, and so on.

Ox gall is actually made from ox bile and acts as a dispersant that allows paints to flow and mix better. It should only be used with organic pigments such as watercolors, gouache, tempera, or pastels and added a drop at a time to mixed paints until the desired effects are achieved.

Marbling tools

Most pigments and paints adapt well to marbling; oil paints, watercolors, pastels, inks, and acrylics are great choices.

No two papers react the same to the marbling process. Almost any paper will work, but some make the paints look more vibrant or textured.

Watercolor paper and rice paper are good choices for water marbling processes. They are very absorbent, and create a matte finish. Craft papers, card stocks, fine linen and cotton papers, as well as chipboard can all be used for marbling, but the results will vary. Again, a little experimentation may be required.

A flat tray, pan, or basin and water are basic marbling tools. When marbling on size solutions, a variety of tools and even household objects can be used to create designs in the paints before printing. Try any of the following: a skewer or chopstick, a long comb with even teeth (some teeth can be broken off to create more space between them), nails pounded through a thin board, a silicone whisk, a fork, an eyedropper, or a toothbrush (for splatters).

Marbling is full of surprises and variations and is always subject to the chemistry involved. The following techniques are samples of the many variations and methods for marbling on paper.

Basic Water Marbling

This method is for watercolors, gouache, or pastels. It is not easy to control the pigments, but the results are still quite amazing.

MATERIALS

■ watercolor paper or rice paper

■ watercolors (no more than two or three colors at a time)

■ mordant solution

■ glass plate or baking dish

Instructions

1 Spray the paper with the mordant solution and allow it to air-dry before continuing.

2 Fill the dish until the bottom is just covered, about ¼" to ½" (6 mm– 1.3 cm) deep with water.

3 Mix all the watercolor paints before starting the rest of the process. The paints should be quite dense.

4 Drop the paints over the water or lightly swirl them in place. Do not try to control the paint too much or it will dilute.

5 Immediately take the paper and press it down to the bottom of the dish until the paper is wet. Quickly lift out starting at one end of the paper.

6 Lay the paper face-up on paper towels and let it dry. The drying process can be accelerated with a heat tool if desired. After the paper is completely dry it can be ironed flat.

VARIATION

For water marbling with pastels, the process is the same. Use a craft knife to lightly scrape the sides of the pastels into dust over the water. Powdered tempera can also be used for this process.

TIPS

▫ Lay the paper over the paints as quickly as possible because the paints will dilute quickly and may flow into each other.

▫ Watercolors are a transparent paint and the results of this type of marbling are not as intense as other processes.

▫ For multicolored effects, the colors can be applied in layers by allowing the paper to dry between color applications.

▫ Rice paper is the most ancient of paper choices for the water marbling processes.

▫ It is not usually necessary to use a mordant when using rice paper and most cold-pressed watercolor papers. These papers are designed to grab water-based pigments. Test the paper if in doubt.

Basic Marbling on Size

This method can be used with any pigment, and is especially well suited for heavier paints such as oil and acrylic. It affords greater control than the water method and the ability to create dramatic patterns.

MATERIALS

- paper
- pigments
- size (thickened water)
- mordant solution
- design tools (combs, picks, eyedroppers, toothbrush)
- marbling tray

Instructions

1 Spray the paper with the mordant solution and allow it to air-dry before continuing.

2 Prepare the size according to the instructions and pour the size ½" to 1" (1.3–2.5 cm) deep into the marbling tray.

3 Test the pigments in a small amount of size to see how they disperse and make any corrections to the viscosity.

4 Splatter or drop the pigments onto the size and manipulate with various tools to create designs.

5 Begin at one end and roll the paper down to prevent air bubbles from getting trapped beneath.

6 Remove the paper from the size by lifting from one end. Hold under a gentle stream of water to remove the size, revealing the print.

7 Allow the paper to air-dry. If needed, the paper can be pressed with a warm iron after it is dry.

MARBLING VARIATIONS

	PROCESS	MORDANT	SIZE	INK	THINNER
	Marbling 1	Alum	Methocel	Marbling Color (Jacquard)	None
	Marbling 2	Alum	Methocel	Acrylic Paints	Water
	Marbling 3	Alum	Carrageenan	Acrylic Paints	Water
	Marbling 4	Alum	Gelatin*	Acrylic Paints	Water
	Marbling 5	Alum	Methocel	Oil Paints	Turpenoid**
	Marbling 6	Alum	Hair Conditioner	Acrylic Paints	Water
	Marbling 7	None	None/Water	Pastels/Chalks	None
	Marbling 8	None	None/Water	Watercolors	Water
	Marbling 9	Alum	Shaving Cream***	Acrylic Paints	Water

*Follow the instructions for the hard-block consistency of gelatin, then add water until the desired consistency is achieved.

**Turpenoid is low-odor turpentine used to thin paints. Work with Turpenoid in a well-ventilated area.

***Smooth the surface of the shaving cream with a bent palette knife before applying the paints.

Luminous Marbling

This process is similar to the Northern Lights (page 54) process except for the final step that adds the textured and marbled effects.

MATERIALS

- paper (black or dark colored)
- Perfect Ink Refresher
- Perfect Pearls (Kiwi, Turquoise, Berry Twist, and Gold)
- paper towel
- paintbrush
- fine-mist spray bottle

Instructions

1 Spray the paper with Perfect Ink Refresher and rub it into the surface gently with a paper towel.
▼

2 Mix each Perfect Pearls color with water to form a creamy paint.

3 Apply the paints randomly in wavy stripes over the paper.
▼

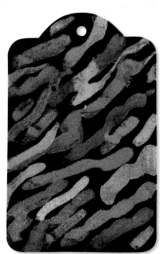

4 Spray with water and then manipulate the paper to make the paints bleed and move. Some water may drip off the edges.
▼

5 While the paper is wet, lightly pounce a crumpled paper towel over the entire surface. This will remove color to create the look of texture and veins.
▼

6 Allow the paper to dry or force the drying with a heat tool.

TIPS

- Rotate the crumpled paper towel every now and then so it doesn't become too saturated with paint.
- Metallic and iridescent paints (watercolor, acrylic, ink, etc) can also be used with most any size-based marbling process to add luminous effects.
- To "pounce" means to tap gently.

ABOUT WATERCOLORS

Watercolor paints are delightful to use because of their unpredictable nature, vibrant colors, and grand effects. As one of the most versatile mediums, it can be used to create spontaneous results or it can be controlled for exacting effects. Watercolors are the most ancient of paints. They are simply pigments mixed with water and a medium, usually gum or glue, which helps them adhere better to paper. As ancient as these paints are, they never cease to intrigue artisans with their creative possibilities.

Thanks to modern technology, watercolor paints are available in a variety of easy-to-use forms such as marking pens, ink pads, crayons, pencils, premixed solutions, sprays, and of course, traditional tubes and cakes. Watercolors can be transparent or opaque. The opaque version, known as *gouache*, is watercolor pigment mixed with titanium white. If the product does not say gouache or opaque, then it is transparent.

Shown clockwise from top: watercolor pencils, tube, crayons, and cakes

WATERCOLOR PAPERS

These papers are made to tolerate water and moisture and to add texture to watercolor painting. The three most common grades of watercolor paper are rough, hot pressed, and cold pressed. Rough paper is just that—it has a heavy tooth (texture) and contributes to the look of the painting the most dramatically. Hot-pressed papers have the smoothest and finest texture. Cold-pressed papers are somewhere in the middle and are the most popular. Cold-pressed papers have a medium tooth and come in many weights. The weight of watercolor paper is expressed in pounds or grams; the higher the number, the thicker the paper. A good general-use watercolor paper weight is 120 lb (176 gsm),

WATERCOLOR BRUSHES

Watercolor brushes are soft, and they come in round and flat shapes and many grades. The best brushes are made of natural fibers and can be very costly, but should last for years with proper care. However, there are many other choices available in every price and grade that will still produce great results. The sizes of brushes are designated by numbers; the higher the number, the larger the brush.

TIP

□ Watercolors dry twice as light in value as they appear when wet.

There are many techniques and methods for using watercolors. This section will cover a few of the most basic and essential techniques plus a few splashy special effects.

Basic Watercolor Washes

Washes are the most basic of watercolor techniques. Watercolor washes are used to cover solid areas with color.

MATERIALS

- watercolor paper
- watercolor paint
- art board or sturdy chipboard
- artist tape
- round watercolor brush (#10 or #12)
- optional: salt, Perfect Pearls

Instructions for Even Washes

1 Tape the watercolor paper to art board or chipboard to keep it from curling.

2 Load the brush with paint. With one stroke, brush a broad stripe of watercolor horizontally at the top of the paper.

Hold the board at a slant so the paint will bleed. A natural puddle of paint will form under the stroke.

3 Load the brush with paint again and position the brush to just touch the previous stroke puddle and make another stroke.

4 Continue this process down the length of the paper. The strokes will bleed together evenly.

Instructions for Graded Washes

1 Tape the watercolor paper to art board or chipboard to stabilize it.

2 Load the brush with paint. With one stroke, brush a broad stripe of watercolor horizontally at the top of the paper. Hold the board at a slant so the paint will bleed. A natural puddle of paint will form under the stroke.

3 Load the brush with water, not paint, position the brush to just touch the previous stroke puddle, and make another stroke. Continue this process down the length of the paper. The paint will get lighter with each stroke.

VARIATIONS

Salt Washes

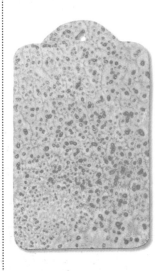

Create a watercolor salt wash by first following the instructions for making any of the washed backgrounds. While the paint is wet, sprinkle it with table salt (or coarse salt for more texture).

Allow the paper to dry completely before brushing the salt off. This method creates beautifully mottled effects.

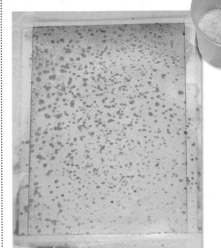

Luminous Watercolors

Artists have a long-standing love affair with all things iridescent, pearly, and luminous: butterfly and fairy wings, sunsets, rainbows, water, metal, shells, and the mysterious lights of day and night, to name a few. Adding a luminous medium to watercolors can create amazing effects that charm the eye and the imagination.

There are liquid luminous pigments available that are designed to mix with watercolors and add that iridescent touch. However, one of the easiest ways to add luminous effects to watercolors is to add Perfect Pearls when mixing the paint. These dry powdered pigments are very fine mica-based pigments with built-in resins and binders so they blend beautifully with watercolors. Add just a pinch to wet paint and mix it in completely.*

TIP

▫ Artist tape is a removable tape that looks like masking tape but won't harm the paper when it is removed. A low-tack masking tape can be used instead.

Watercolor Plastic Wrap Treatment

This method creates a batik effect with variegations and shapes that can only be achieved with watercolors. It is very simple but looks like intricate brush and masking work. Every plastic wrap print will be unique. This process can't be controlled, so enjoy the spontaneity.

MATERIALS

- watercolor paper
- watercolor paint
- art board or sturdy chipboard
- artist tape
- plastic wrap
- round watercolor brush (#10 or #12)

Instructions

1 Follow the instructions for making any of the washed backgrounds.

2 While the paint is wet, lay the board flat, wrinkle the plastic wrap, and press into the watercolor.

▶

3 Allow the paper to dry completely before removing the plastic wrap to reveal the design.

TIP

▫ Try this method using several colors at a time.

Watercolor Staining

This technique is used to create subtle effects that are controlled in a specific area. A shape or image can be placed in the middle of the paper and the paint will stay confined to the prepared area without masking.

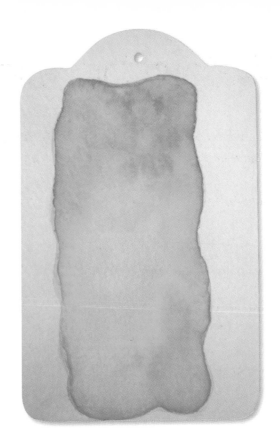

MATERIALS

- watercolor paper
- watercolor paint
- art board or sturdy chipboard
- artist tape
- round watercolor brush (#10 or #12)

Unlike washes, staining is typically done layer upon layer to give the image depth. This method is often used to create shadows and give painted objects dimension. It makes a great background for stamped images and calligraphy because it defines the area.

Instructions

1 Tape the watercolor paper to art board or chipboard to keep it from curling.

2 Paint the shape or area on the paper with water. While the paper is wet, pick up paint on the end of the brush and lightly touch the brush in the wet area.

▼

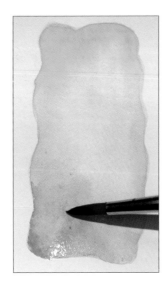

The paint will flow from the brush and bleed onto the paper but will stay confined to the wet area.

3 To intensify the colors, wait until the first application is completely dry and then repeat the process by painting over the area with water and then adding more color. This process can be repeated many times, but the paper must be completely dry between applications.

TIPS

- Do this process with good lighting so it is easy to see where the water is being laid.
- To make the water easier to see for the initial application of water, add a very small amount of paint to tint the water slightly.
- Resist overworking. The paint and water will work together if left alone to fill the area and make natural shading.

Watercolor Pencils

*Use watercolor pencils the same way as ordinary pencils.
Hold them, sharpen them, and erase them in the same way.
However, the major difference is that the pigment in watercolor
pencils is water-soluble paint that becomes fluid when wet.*

MATERIALS

- watercolor paper
- watercolor pencils
- art board or sturdy chipboard
- artist tape
- craft knife
- round watercolor brush (#10 or #12)

There are several ways to free the paint from a watercolor pencil. One way is to simply draw, then apply clean water with a brush and watch the paints come to life. Another way is to wet the paper first and then lightly draw on it. The pencil marks will spread upon contact. Shaving watercolor lead by scraping it with a craft knife over wet paper produces vibrant splatter effects, with very little bleeding. Try dampening the tip of the pencil and then drawing to create more dense colors.

Paint can also be lifted from the pencil by stroking a wet brush on the pencil tip to gather color.

Watercolor pencils offer some very unique design possibilities and can be used to add detail and shading to most any watercolor painting.

Instructions

1 Tape the watercolor paper to art board or chipboard to keep it from curling.

2 Follow the instructions for making any of the washed backgrounds.

3 While the paint is wet, use a craft knife to shave color flecks from a watercolor pencil onto the paper.

▼

□ To make watercolor pencils luminous, mix a small amount of pearl Perfect Pearls with water to form a thin paint. Use this to cure the pencil instead of plain water.

Watercolor Masking Techniques

Masking is simply the act of covering up portions of the paper so paint will not be deposited there. The mask is later removed to reveal the original surface. Masking can create depth and dimension on a flat piece of paper. It can also preserve the color of the paper as part of the composition, such as masking on white, which later becomes the white parts of the piece. These techniques are loads of fun and there are lots of ways to mask paper.

MATERIALS

- ▩ watercolor paper
- ▩ watercolor paint
- ▩ masking fluid
- ▩ artist tape
- ▩ art board or sturdy chipboard
- ▩ medium round watercolor brush

Most art stores carry art masking fluid, which is used in the technique shown here. Masking fluid, which is applied wet, dries to a rubbery consistency that rubs off easily when the painting process is complete. If the masking fluid is difficult to remove, solvents are available that will not damage the painting.

Instructions

1 Tape the watercolor paper to hard art board or chipboard to keep it from curling.

2 Apply masking fluid and let dry.

3 Paint the watercolors over the mask by following the instructions for making any of the washed backgrounds.
▼

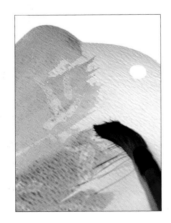

4 Gently rub off the mask using a fingertip.
▼

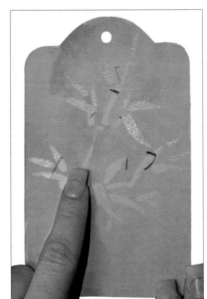

VARIATIONS

Creative Masking Techniques

Several options and products are available for masking.

Artist release tape is available through art stores and is used to tape paper to boards where it can be removed without damaging the paper. It is also used to create masked borders and geometric lines in compositions. It is typically 1" to 1½" (2.5–3.8 cm) wide.

Eclipse is an art masking tape that is 6" (15.2 cm) wide, making it possible to die-cut, punch, or cut custom shapes for masking. It comes on a 33' (10 m) roll so it can be cut into long sections.

Most hardware stores carry an easy-release masking tape. Test it on the paper to be sure the tape won't damage the paper.

Rubber cement glue, although stinky, can be used to mask with and is very easy to rub off. This is an inexpensive alternative to artist masking flu-

ids but is not as easy to apply precisely because of its thicker consistency.

It is always fun to create custom shapes for masking. Try using die cuts, punched shapes, decorative-edge scissor strips, custom shapes, and stencils. Use a removable adhesive to make custom shapes stick temporarily for the painting process. Cut these masks from sturdy paper so they stand up to the painting process. Also test the paper for color fastness to be sure it won't bleed if it becomes wet.

Water Webbing

Imagine tiny threads of color vibrating from the paint source—that's what water webbing has to offer. It is a delicate effect that seems to create vibrations and draws the eye to its source. This technique can be done with most water-based paints or inks, except archival and permanent pigments, which are designed to resist bleeding when wet. It is also a beautiful method to use with stamps. Choose a soft, cold-pressed watercolor paper that is 120 lb (176 gsm) or heavier for this treatment. Some card stock will work if it is soft and more absorbent. Do not use hot-pressed or glossy papers. For stamping, choose bold images without a lot of fine-lined detail. Use watercolor (also called dye-based or water-based) inks for this process. Do not use pigment or embossing inks.

MATERIALS

- watercolor paper (120 lb [176 gsm])
- water-based ink
- artist tape
- art board or sturdy chipboard
- bold-lined image stamp
- spray bottle
- optional: brush

Instructions

1 Tape the watercolor paper to art board or chipboard to keep it from curling.

2 Lightly mist the paper with water and wipe off any excess moisture.

3 Press the stamp ▶ firmly into the ink to pick up as much ink as possible and stamp onto the paper.

4 Remove the stamp ▶ and immediately spray with water from the spray bottle. Hold the bottle 8" to 10" (20–25 cm) directly over the image. Spray just once or the image will lose detail. The pressure from applying the water will move the paint into the webbing patterns.

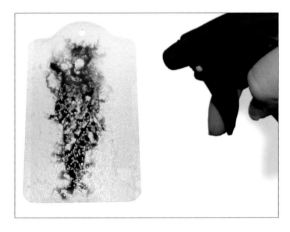

TIPS

- For added punch, dust the image with Perfect Pearls while it is still damp and the webbing will pick up a luminous glow.

- For more subtle effects, blot the image with a paper towel.

VARIATION

Apply watercolor paints directly to the paper with a brush instead of using a stamp.

TIP

- When using this technique for painting, try laying a webbed background, and when it is dry, go back into it with more detail.

Mottled Paper

These papers conjure up imaginings of painting in the open air and being surprised by a sudden and brief rain shower. After a mad dash to safety, it's discovered that a newly color-washed watercolor was left out. As it turns out, the piece will turn into a work of art while in the hands of nature. The washed background is now peppered with soft splatters of defined color, telling where every drop landed. It's so hard not to be romantic about these papers! This is a beautiful paper for bookmakers and can easily take the place of marbled endpapers. However, rather than waiting for a rain shower, the effects of water splatters on watercolor pigment is quite easy to reproduce. Here are a few easy methods.

MATERIALS

- glossy or matte paper
- water-based pigments
- artist tape
- art board or sturdy chipboard
- paper towel
- spray bottle

Instructions

1 Create a solid background of water-based pigments on watercolor paper, glossy paper, or card stock. Any of the following methods will work:
- Use a brayer to roll water-based ink from an ink pad.

- Spray the paper with watercolor sprays.
- Apply a traditional watercolor wash.
- Use watercolor pencils or watercolor crayons.
- Use a "direct-to-paper" technique and apply the ink from the pad or with sponge applicators.

2 Hold a spray bottle about 8" to 10" (20–25 cm) directly over the piece and spray water over it.
▼

3 Use a paper towel to blot excess moisture; don't rub or it will smear. It will dry with beautiful splatter marks.
▼

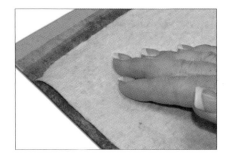

TIP
▫ For best results, use a spray bottle that creates droplets and not a fine mist.

▫ Sometimes the paper towel is the work of art! Try using tissue paper to blot with. These papers make great collage papers.

▼

▫ When using matte paper or card stock for this process, the ink will disperse more than it does on glossy paper, creating softer effects.

▼

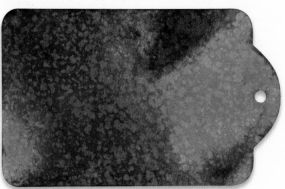

Watercolor Sprays

Spraying watercolor is just plain-old dreamy! This method can produce quick and interesting backgrounds with tons of special effects. Just put mixed watercolors in a small spray bottle and they're ready to use. Every sprayer bottle will produce a different spray; some produce a very fine mist while others are good for splattering treatments. It will take a little practice to get to know a sprayer. This process creates paper with speckled and grainy effects and makes wonderful backdrops for layered processes.

MATERIALS

■ watercolor paper or card stock

■ watercolors

■ artist tape

■ art board or sturdy chipboard

■ spray bottles

There are also water-based transparent sprays available that have more intense color and are permanent after drying or setting with heat. Whatever the choice, they act similarly when wet and are great fun to use. These methods are not very controllable, which means every piece is a unique work of art—a trademark of most water-based processes.

Do these techniques on wet or dry paper. Wet paper will result in a more blended look while dry paper will show the splattering more.

Backgrounds can be one color or multiple colors. Simply start spraying. If the colors start blending or getting muddy, use a crumpled paper towel to lightly pat the excess color and moisture off the paper. This will create subtle variations in the paint. Pressing lightly on the spray pumper will often give the best splattering.

Instructions

1 Tape the watercolor paper to art board or chipboard to keep it from curling.

2 Mix the watercolors and put them in to small spray bottles.

3 Hold the spray bottle 8" to 10" (20–25 cm) directly over the paper and spray the color onto the paper. Repeat with more colors if desired.
▼

VARIATIONS

To create raindrop effects (mottling), apply base color(s) and allow it to dry, then spray clear water over the top, let it rest for a few seconds and then blot (don't rub) with a paper towel.
▶

Try masking an area and then spraying with color. Remove the masks and spray the uncolored areas. (For more on masking, see page 25.)

TIP

▫ For an even wash over the paper, spray the paper with water and wipe off the excess moisture. Spray with color and use a rubber brayer to distribute the paint. This will create a more even distribution of color.

ABOUT PASTE PAPER

There is something special about a design that can be perceived both visually and by touch. Paste paper brings an extra dimension to the flat world of paper by providing physical texture. For centuries it has been used to create lavish wall coverings and distinctive papers.

Paste paper is made by applying a thick paste medium to paper and raking or stamping in it to create patterns. It is called paste because it is traditionally a medium that bonds to paper. There are many ways to make paste and many art supply products that will create beautiful textural effects on paper. This section includes two vintage recipes and some exciting new variations for making and creating with paste paper.

Paste can be used plain or tinted with pigments. To add color, put the paste into a small mixing cup and add a drop at a time of acrylic paint, watercolor, ink, or other compatible pigments and mix well.

□ Spread the paste over the paper using a bent palette knife.

▼

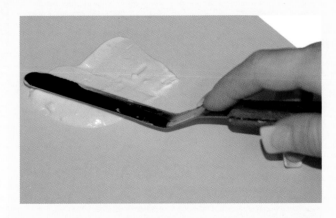

□ If the paper is not sturdy, tape it to a piece of chipboard or art board with low-tack tape, then apply the paste. Allow the paper to air-dry before removing it from the board.

□ If the paper wrinkles after it dries, lightly mist the back with water and press with a warm iron to flatten.

□ Try spreading paste over printed and patterned papers with a palette knife.

▼

□ To create custom texture, rake with a fork or other tool (combs, chopsticks, etc).

▼

□ Stamping also creates beautiful effects in paste paper. Try using the paste plain and stamping into it. This makes beautiful textural tone-on-tone effects. When stamping onto paste, be sure to wash the stamp promptly so the paste does not harden on the stamp.

▼

□ To use paste with stencils, use a low-tack tape to stabilize the stencil and then apply the paste with a palette knife.

▼

□ Carefully remove the stencil while the paste is still wet.

▼

□ Add mica powdered pigments or glitter to pastes for even more punch.

Traditional Cooked Cornstarch Paste

This is an ancient method that uses simple ingredients and makes a superior paste medium. It is more translucent than wheat paste and very creamy. Adding water-based pigments to this paste creates textural watercolor effects. Adding acrylic paints will make the paste more opaque. Oil colors cannot be added to this paste.

MATERIALS

- water (2½ cups [590 ml])
- cornstarch (⅓ cup [40 g])
- optional: white glue, cream of tartar

Instructions

1 Combine the water and cornstarch and heat to boiling while stirring constantly.

2 After the mixture comes to a boil, turn the heat down and cook over low heat while it thickens. It will turn grayish in color and become more translucent as it cooks. When thick, remove the paste from the heat and allow it to cool.

3 When the paste is cool, use a spatula to press it through a strainer or squeeze the mixture through cheesecloth to remove any lumps (this can be a messy process).

4 Add pigments to color the paste. Allow it to cool and use the paste immediately.

VARIATION

Add 1 tablespoon (15 ml) of white paper glue and ½ teaspoon (2.5 ml) of cream of tartar to the paste for added stability and a more creamy texture.

TIPS

▫ Cornstarch paste can curl the paper while it is drying, so tape the paper to an art board or sturdy chipboard and remove it after it is completely dry.

▫ The paste can be stored in the refrigerator for a few days, but it is best to use it immediately.

▫ Cornstarch paste can be used to produce fine lines, sometimes called *cracklique*, which makes a piece look cracked and aged. To create crackle finishes, paint a light coat of cornstarch paste on the paper and allow it to air-dry. When the paper is dry, manipulate it until the dried paste cracks on the surface. Misting the back of the paper with water and pressing it flat on the back with a warm iron will also create fine lines.

Jelly Paste

This paste looks and spreads like smooth jelly and dries fairly translucent. It is a modern twist on the Traditional Cooked Cornstarch Paste recipe.

MATERIALS

- cornstarch paste (1 cup [240 ml])
- Glossy Accents or a clear gel acrylic medium (1 tablespoon [15 ml])
- transparent pigment (watercolors, inks, or transparent dyes)

Instructions

1 Make traditional cornstarch paste (see page 32).

2 When it is cool, add 1 tablespoon (15 ml) of Glossy Accents or a clear gel acrylic medium to the paste. Add color and use the paste immediately. This paste does not store well.

Traditional Cooked Wheat Paste

This is another ancient process for making paper glue. It is more opaque than the cornstarch recipe. It is an excellent medium for adding pigments and can be thinned with water if needed. Water-based pigments such as watercolors, acrylics, and inks are the best choice for adding color to this paste. Wheat paste can be stored for a few days in the refrigerator, but beware of mold. Make the paste fresh and use it immediately whenever possible.

MATERIALS

- bleached white flour (1 cup [120 g])
- water (1½ cups [355 ml])
- optional: white glue, cream of tartar

Instructions

1 Combine the water and flour and heat over low heat, stirring constantly, until the paste thickens. If the paste cooks too quickly and seems to be getting hard, remove it from the heat and continue stirring.

When the lumps have been worked out, return to the heat until the right consistency is achieved. Remove the paste from the heat and allow it to cool. More water can be added for a thinner paste.

2 When the paste is cool, use a rubber spatula to press it through a strainer to remove any lumps (this can be a messy process).

3 Add pigments to color the paste and use the paste immediately.

VARIATIONS

Add ½ teaspoon (2.5 ml) of cream of tartar to the flour before the cooking process to make the paste creamier. Add 1 tablespoon (15 ml) of white glue, Glossy Accents, or any gel acrylic medium to the paste when it is cooled for added stability.

Luminous Paste

Luminous paste paper makes an elegant statement on any project.

MATERIALS

- paper
- Glossy Accents
- Perfect Pearls or any powdered luminous pigment
- plastic fork
- optional: glitter

Instructions

1 Mix Perfect Pearls with a little water to form a very thick creamy paint. Add Glossy Accents until the right consistency for the paste is achieved. This mixture can be thinned with a few drops of water.

2 Quickly spread the paste on the paper with a palette knife and rake it with a plastic fork to create texture. Allow the paper to dry completely before using it.

TIPS

- Perfect Pearls are ideal for this paste because they have built-in binders, which make the medium thicker. They also contain a slight amount of pigment along with fine mica particles, so the effects are quite brilliant.
- Use a palette knife or a wide craft stick to apply the paste to the paper and texturize immediately.
- Avoid overworking the paste or the colors can get muddy.

VARIATIONS

For more sparkle, glitter can be added to the mixture or sprinkled on top while the paste is wet. Perfect Sparkles make gorgeous paste papers because they have mica glitter already in them.

SUBSTITUTION

Gel acrylic medium can be used to make a luminous paste instead of Glossy Accents, to which any powdered mica pigment can be added. Gel acrylic medium can also be thinned with water.

Spackle Paste

This is a very smooth yet highly textured paste. It blends well with any water-based pigment and is extremely sturdy after it dries. This paste creates great architectural effects.

MATERIALS

■ card stock or paper

■ exterior spackling paste (½ cup [120 ml])

■ polymer medium (2 tablespoons [30 ml])

■ water-based ink or paint (acrylic, watercolors, re-inkers, etc)

■ palette knife or spatula

■ raking tool (comb, stick, fork, etc)

Instructions

1 In a small mixing cup, mix the spackling paste with the polymer medium until well blended. Add water to make the paste thinner if desired.

2 To color the paste, add paint or ink by the drop and mix well.

3 Apply the paste to the paper with the palette knife. Spread the paste on the paper until the desired thickness is achieved.

4 Pull the raking tool through the paste in the vertical direction then again in a horizontal direction. The raking of the paste can be done a variety of ways to create different patterns.

5 Allow the paste to air-dry. Once the paste paper is dry, additional highlights of color may be added by rubbing the piece with paints or inks.

TIP

□ Be sure to use exterior spackle because it is water-resistant after it dries and more stable than interior spackle.

Splatter Effects

Splattering makes wonderful aged effects or suggests pure abandon and exuberance. The famous painter Jackson Pollock achieved fame from his splattered paintings. Almost any painting medium can be splattered unless it is too thick. Every artist has to discover the technique that works best from the many ingenious methods.

MATERIALS

■ paper or card stock
■ paint
■ splattering tool

Instructions

1 Dip the splattering tool into the paint and flick it onto the paper or card stock.

SPLATTERING TOOLS

• Silicone basting brushes make excellent splatter tools, but the paint can fly, so take precautions with an apron and drop cloth. This method makes large splatters. ▶

• A toothbrush works well but it can get the finger-nails and hands messy, so use gloves if that doesn't appeal. The effects will be a small-scale and compressed splatter. ▶

• There are several tools available through art stores, such as a spool and wire brush or a screen and wire brush.

• Marbling artists often use bundles of broom twigs or fine branch twigs for splattering.

ABOUT PASTELS

Many of the paintings produced by the great impressionist painter Edgar Degas were painted with pastels (think of all those pretty ballerinas!). Needless to say, pastels are a respected fine art medium, but crafters and paper artists have discovered their versatility and they have never been more popular.

Pastels come in two varieties: oil-based and "soft" (or dry) pigment pastels. The lesser grades are considered chalks. They range in value from "pastel" to vibrant. As with any art pigment, pastels come in many grades and price ranges and the quality of the pigments can differ dramatically. Excluding those specific to oil pastels, the following techniques work well for all types of pastels and chalks.

OIL PASTELS

These vibrant oil paints have a wax binder and come in paper-wrapped sticks. They are applied directly from the stick or color is lifted with a brush or tool.  They are soft and easy to blend. Oil pastels can be lifted and thinned with turpentine. Rubber color shapers and other instruments can be used to manipulate these pigments.

SOFT PASTELS

Soft pastels are dry pigment that come in sticks or pencils and have an inert binder that serves to keep the sticks from falling apart. They can be shaded and manipulated on the paper by using a variety of blending tools. For the best results, use this type of pastel on pastel or charcoal papers because these papers have a soft tooth that grab the pigments well. ▼

CRAFT CHALKS

Chalks are also dry pigments that are very soft and were originally made from pure chalk bases. Now they come in cakes and are a favorite of crafters because of their wide range of vibrant colors, luminous colors, and custom collections. They are easy to use with an applicator, and a little goes a long way. Craft chalks are not all created equal, so choose a good quality chalk with rich pigments that keep their intensity.

APPLYING PASTELS AND CHALKS

Pastels come in sticks and pencils and are simple to apply, but chalks are popular in cakes and require an applicator that comes with most chalks. Cotton balls or pom-poms used with an alligator clip are also a popular choice. Cotton swabs and soft felt will also work. ▼

STABILIZING SOFT PASTELS AND CHALKS

The biggest challenge to using soft pastels and chalks is preserving the finished artwork. Soft pastels and chalks are dry pigment and can easily be rubbed off, so fixatives are used to preserve them. There are "workable" fixatives that stabilize the pigments during the creative process and allow them to be reworked and erased if necessary. Apply a permanent fixative as a final topcoat. Most art stores carry spray fixatives but they are not all acid free, which can be a concern for scrapbook artists. If there are no concerns about the acid-free nature or about using aerosols, try aerosol hairspray as a fixative, but test it before applying it to the entire project.

The paper can also be treated with a special medium that will act as a fixative. Perfect Medium is an artist medium used in stamping. It can be rubbed evenly in to the paper surface before the chalks are applied. The chalks will set permanently after they are applied, and this process is archival safe and acid free. It also keeps the chalk colors vibrant.

TOOLS

There are many tools that are used with pastels, including rolled paper blending stumps, rubber color shapers, alligator clips with cotton balls, cotton swabs, and kneaded erasers. Kneaded erasers are great because they can be shaped and work well for lifting color and making corrections.

TIP

□ Use medium-grade sandpaper to clean or sharpen a rolled paper blending stump.

Pastel Layering and Masking Techniques

This is a great method for creating water and sky effects as well as perspective. Use a torn scrap of paper, or a die cut or custom shape as a mask.

MATERIALS

- paper or card stock
- soft pastels or chalk
- die cut
- fixative
- pastel applicator

Instructions

1 Place the die cut on the paper or card stock.

2 Apply the pastels in a swiping motion from the die cut to the paper.

3 Move the die cut to another spot on the paper and repeat the process.

4 Apply fixative as a final topcoat unless the paper was pretreated.

TIPS

- □ Use a repositionable adhesive to hold masks in place.
- □ Soft pastels and chalks come in luminous and pearly versions. Use these like any soft pastels or chalks.
- □ To make any pastel glimmer, prep the paper with Perfect Medium and apply Perfect Pearls after the pastel pigments have been applied. This produces a luminous sheen over the entire piece.

Shading with Pastels

Pastels are a wonderful choice to color stamped images, shade die-cut shapes, or to give paper added dimension.

MATERIALS

- die cut
- pastel pigments
- fixative
- pastel applicator

Instructions

1 Apply the pastels to the die cut and use pastels or chalks to create shading, depth, and visual interest.

►

2 Apply a fixative as a final topcoat unless the paper was pretreated.

Pastels and Stamps

This is an easy technique that allows pastels to be used with stamping. Simply stamp using Perfect Medium and lightly dust or pat pastels over the image. The medium will pick up the chalks and fix them. The paper around the stamped image will also pick up the pastels, but will be more muted than the stamped image.

MATERIALS

- paper or card stock
- soft pastels or chalk
- Perfect Medium
- stamp (Stampers Anonymous, U1-846)
- pastel applicator
- brush
- optional: Perfect Pearls, fine-mist spray bottle

Instructions

1 Stamp an image using Perfect Medium.

2 Apply pastels or chalk to the stamped image by tapping it on with an applicator. Use a larger brush to "dust" off any excess pigment.
▶

VARIATION

After applying the soft pastels or chalk, use a brush to dust Perfect Pearls over the image. This will add a luminous effect to only the image.
▶

Set the Perfect Pearls pigments with a light mist of water.

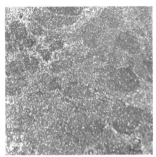

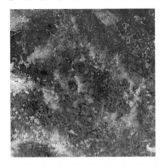
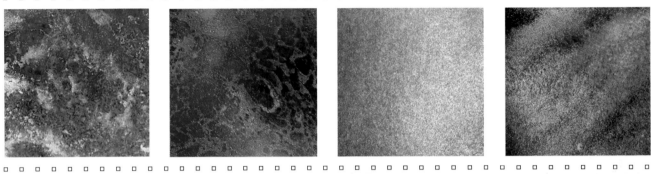

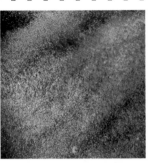

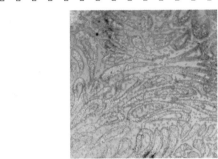
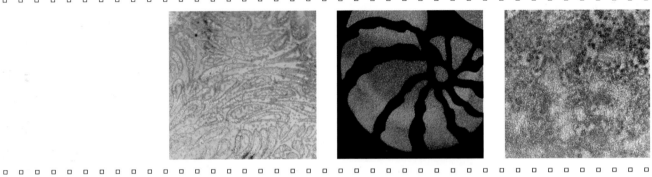
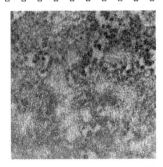

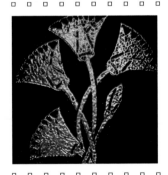
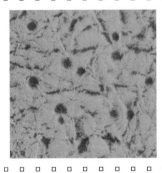
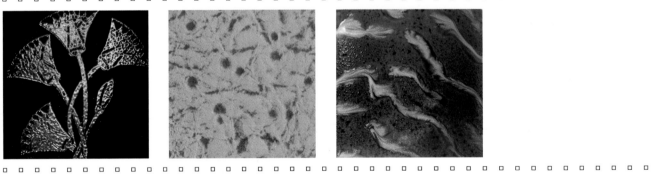

CHAPTER TWO

Original Designer Papers

Creating original designer papers not only adds a touch of true distinction to any creative project, but it also brings out the "mad scientist" in an artist. Experimenting with papers, mediums, and techniques can be an exciting discovery process. It's amazing what effects can be achieved from using just a few simple craft supplies and a lot of imagination.

Some of the papers in this chapter were inspired by actual surfaces while others were the result of fun experimentation. While experimenting, try to think outside of the box and use mediums in ways that are unfamiliar or seem unique. Write your successful experiments down so they can be duplicated and shared in the future.

This type of creative play is very rewarding and the results are a limitless variety of original papers. Beware, this process can be addicting!

Leather Paper

This paper treatment creates the look of real leather. The Perfect Ink Refresher conditions the paper by making it soft and flexible during the design process. Leather paper can be molded to cover books, boxes, and three-dimensional objects. This paper will stiffen again after it has dried.

MATERIALS

- card stock (leatherlike color)
- Perfect Ink Refresher
- iron
- optional: dye-based ink, Perfect Pearls, brush, iron

Instructions

1 Spray the card stock on both sides with Perfect Ink Refresher and gently rub onto the paper.
▼

2 Crumple the paper repeatedly until the desired texture is achieved. If the paper will be used to cover a three-dimensional object, now is the time to apply it.
▼

3 If the paper is to be used flat, iron flat to dry.
▼

VARIATIONS

To accent the leather, glide dye-based ink lightly over the paper to deepen the contrast of the fine lines after completing step 2.
▶

To create luminous leather paper, lightly brush Perfect Pearls over the paper after step 2 but before ironing.
▶

Ostrich Leather Paper

This leather is distinctive because of its inherent dots. The process is very similar to faux Leather Paper until the final steps.

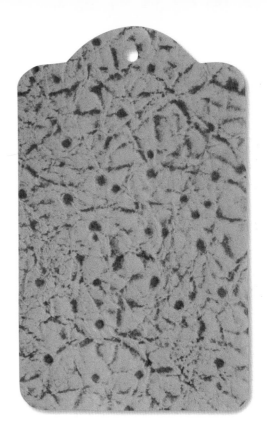

MATERIALS

- card stock
- dye-based ink
- Perfect Ink Refresher
- paper towel
- fine-mist spray bottle
- brush
- iron
- foam (mouse pad)

Instructions

1 Spray the card stock on both sides with Perfect Ink Refresher and gently rub onto the paper.

2 Crumple the paper repeatedly until the desired texture is achieved.

3 Iron the paper flat.

4 Lightly mist the paper on both sides with water and wipe it off with a paper towel. This small amount of moisture will keep the paper from fracturing during the next step.

5 Lay the paper on the foam and lightly press indents into it using the handle of the brush.
▼

6 Iron the paper flat from the side it was pounded on.
▼

7 Lightly rub a dye-based ink pad over the front of the paper.
▼

Cosmos Paper

This process involves an unusual way to use extra-thick embossing powder. The result is a glossy, multidimensional effect that draws the eye in to the colorful layers.

MATERIALS

- illustration board or card stock (glue together three to five layers of white card stock)
- pigments (pigment inks, dye-based inks, markers, watercolors, or colored pencils)
- extra-thick embossing powder (clear Ultra Thick Embossing Enamel [UTEE])
- Perfect Medium
- Perfect Pearls (Gold, Kiwi, Berry Twist)
- brush
- heat gun
- optional: plastic fork

Instructions

1 Color the illustration board.

▼

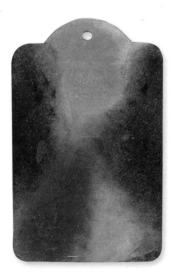

Note: If the piece has been colored with pigment inks, continue with the next step. If another coloring method was used, apply Perfect Medium or embossing ink first so the UTEE will stick, then continue with the process.

2 Pour UTEE liberally over the entire piece. Heat until the surface is smooth, and while it is still hot, sprinkle more UTEE on and keep heating. When this layer is melted and while it is still hot, sprinkle the surface with UTEE one more time and heat until it is melted.

The results will be a very glossy, glasslike finish. Let the piece cool completely before continuing.

▼

3 Apply Perfect Medium to the piece. This will put an oily coating over the surface.

▼

4 Lightly brush on Perfect Pearls.

▶

5 Sprinkle UTEE on top of the Perfect Pearl layer (there won't be anything to make the embossing powder stick) and begin heating from a distance so the embossing powder won't blow away. The embossing powder will become tacky and the heat tool can slowly be moved in closer. The UTEE on the surface will ball up, and as the bottom layers heat they will drop in to the rest of the layers, creating trails of luminous colors and revealing the colors beneath in places.

▶

VARIATION

To create marbled cosmos paper, wait a few seconds immediately after step 5, and then rake a plastic fork or other tool over the piece. This will marble the colors and leave some texture.

▶

TIPS

▫ Consider using Perfect Pearls interference colors; because they are transparent, they are particularly beautiful in this process.

▫ This process is best done in areas smaller than 4" × 4" (10.2 × 10.2 cm).

Faux Sea Glass

This process produces the look of weathered sea glass. It can also be done on glass, wood, or metal. To create the look of sea glass, choose colors that are muted and soft. To produce the look of pitted glass or rock, use more vibrant colors. The process is the same as for Cosmos Paper until the last step.

MATERIALS

- illustration board or mat board (white or cream)
- pigments (pigment inks, dye-based inks, markers, watercolors, or colored pencils)
- extra-thick embossing powder (clear Ultra Thick Embossing Enamel [UTEE])
- Perfect Medium
- Perfect Pearls (Gold, Kiwi, Berry Twist)
- brush
- heat gun
- spray bottle

Instructions

1 Color the illustration board. **Note:** If the piece has been colored with pigment inks, continue with the next step. If another coloring method was used, apply Perfect Medium or embossing ink first so the UTEE will stick, then continue with the process.

▼

2 Pour UTEE liberally over the entire piece. Heat until the surface is smooth, and while it is still hot, sprinkle more UTEE on and keep heating. When this layer is melted and while it is still hot, sprinkle the surface with UTEE one more time and heat until it is melted. The results will be a very glossy, glasslike finish. Let the piece cool completely before continuing.

▼

3 Apply Perfect Medium to the piece. This will put an oily coating over the surface.

▼

4 Lightly brush on Perfect Pearls.
▼

5 Sprinkle UTEE on top of the Perfect Pearls layer (there won't be anything to make the embossing powder stick) and begin heating from a distance so the embossing powder won't blow away. The embossing powder will become tacky and the heat tool can slowly be moved in closer. The UTEE on the surface will ball up, and as the bottom layers heat they will drop in to the rest of the layers, creating trails of luminous colors and revealing the colors beneath in places. ▶

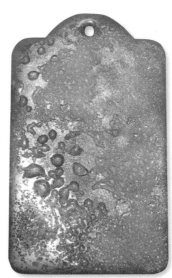

6 Remove the heat and immediately spray with water to pit the surface.
▼

Shining Stones

This is a simple water-based process that produces the look of luminously veined marble and colorful polished stones. Use this paper to create the look of marble on flat surfaces. You can also stamp, emboss, write, or print on it.

MATERIALS

- glossy card stock
- dye-based ink
- Perfect Pearls (Gold)
- paper towel
- brush
- brayer
- fine-mist spray bottle

TIP

□ Work quickly for the best results. Any Perfect Pearls color will work for this process.

Instructions

1 Use a brayer to liberally apply the dye-based ink to the glossy paper. Load the paper with ink even though it may not be able to absorb it all.
▼

2 Mix Perfect Pearls with water to form a creamy paint.

3 Mist the paper with water.
▼

4 Use a small brush to quickly make wavy stripes of gold paint over the surface.
▼

5 Mist again with water and immediately use a crumpled paper towel to gently dab and twist on the surface, creating the look of texture and veins. Allow to dry completely before using.
▼

Luminous Dusting

Here is a simple way to add glowing effects to any paper project. This process can be used with stamps or freehanded.

MATERIALS

■ matte paper (black or dark colored)

■ Perfect Medium

■ Perfect Pearls

■ stamp

■ fine-mist spray bottle

■ brushes (two sizes)

■ optional: Perfect Medium pen, stencil

Instructions

1 Stamp a design using Perfect Medium.

▼

2 Pick up a small amount of the Perfect Pearls pigment powder on a brush and apply to the stamped image. Use a larger brush to dust off the excess powder.

▼ ▼

3 Set the image by spritzing once with a fine mist of water.

▼

VARIATIONS

Perfect Medium comes in a pen, making it easy to produce beautiful luminous writing or freehand work. This is also a great process to use with stencils and templates.

TIPS

- Use matte paper for this process; it will not work on glossy papers.

- Perfect Medium comes in a black-colored pad and pen that are used to create more contrast on lighter colored papers.

Luminous Lifting

Any stamped image can be "lifted" from a luminous background with this process. This look is opposite the look achieved from Luminous Dusting. Featured alongside each other, these papers create a dramatic contrast.

MATERIALS

- paper (black or dark colored)
- Perfect Medium
- Perfect Pearls
- paper towel or sponge
- stamp
- brushes (two sizes)
- fine-mist spray bottle

Instructions

1 Rub Perfect Medium into the paper with a paper towel or a sponge.

▶

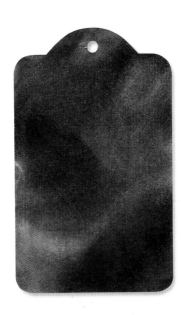

2 Apply Perfect Pearls with a brush and use a larger brush to dust off the excess powder.

3 Press the stamp into the Perfect Medium and stamp onto the luminous background. The image will be "lifted" (removed) from the background.

4 Set with a mist of water.

TIPS

- If multiple stamp images are desired, clean the stamp between each stamping.

- A solid shape or a "shadow" stamp may be used to create the background. Use Perfect Medium to stamp the background then continue the process.

Pearly Mottled Paper

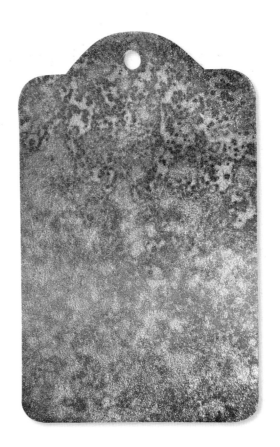

Dye-based inks or watercolors make the background for this beautiful paper that looks like it was left out in a luminous rain shower. Similar to the Mottled Paper process, Pearly Mottled Paper uses Perfect Pearls to increase the drama. The process can be a little unpredictable because every paper absorbs color and dries differently. A little practice is all it takes to make this visually striking paper.

MATERIALS

- paper (white or light colored)
- dye-based ink pad (rainbow)
- Perfect Pearls (Kiwi, Gold)
- paper towel
- brayer
- spray bottle
- brush
- optional: water-based markers, watercolors

Instructions

1 Use a brayer to apply the dye-based ink to the paper.

2 Hold the squirt bottle 8" to 10" (20–25 cm) directly over the paper and spray once or twice just to make water splatters on the paper. Blot (don't rub) with a paper towel. Allow the paper to dry for a few moments, but not too long as some moisture is needed for the rest of the process.

3 While the paper is slightly wet, apply the Perfect Pearls with a brush. The Perfect Pearls pigments will cling to the damp areas and set themselves.

VARIATION

Water-based markers or watercolors can be used to make the background for this process. Allow the water to puddle for a minute before blotting if watercolors are being used.

TIPS

- Apply a moderate amount of ink. If applied too heavily, it can dull the contrast.
- Use a spray bottle that squirts droplets and not a bottle that sprays a mist.

Northern Lights

The Aurora borealis has some competition with this paper. The paper is preconditioned to resist these brilliant paints and some magical effects can be achieved from manipulating the paper to create movement. No two papers will ever be exactly alike. This can be an addictive process!

MATERIALS

- paper (black or dark colored)
- Perfect Ink Refresher
- Perfect Pearls (Kiwi, Turquoise, Berry Twist, Gold)
- paper towel
- brush
- fine-mist spray bottle
- optional: heat tool

Instructions

1 Spray the paper with Perfect Ink Refresher and rub into the surface gently with a paper towel. Repeat if desired.

▼

2 Mix each Perfect Pearls color with water to form a creamy paint.

3 Apply the paints randomly in wavy stripes over the paper.

▼

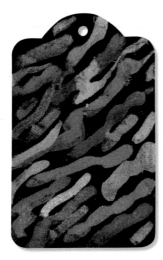

4 Spray with water and then manipulate the paper to make the paints bleed and move. Some water may drip off the edges. Allow the paper to dry or force the drying with a heat tool.

▼

TIPS

- If the paper has buckled during the process it can be ironed flat after it is dry.

- Glycerin or a clear embossing ink can sometimes be substituted for the Perfect Ink Refresher. Experiment a little. The goal is to set up a barrier so the paints will run and bleed and not soak into the paper too quickly.

- The binders in the Perfect Pearls will act like a fixative when the paints are dry.

Shimmer Paper

This process will turn any paper into a soft shimmering version of itself. The glaze should be mixed thin or interference colors should be used (which are transparent) so the paper color is not masked.

MATERIALS

- card stock
- Perfect Pearls
- paper towel
- brush

TIP
▫ To make warm tones, use the gold Perfect Pearls. To make cool tones, use the pearl Perfect Pearls.

Instructions

1 Mix Perfect Pearls with water to form a thin paint. The transparency of the glaze will depend on how much water is added.
▼

2 Quickly paint over the paper, stroking in both directions.
▼

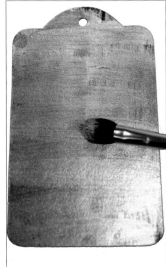

3 Immediately buff with a paper towel in a circular motion. The finish should be completely smooth and even without brushstokes.
▼

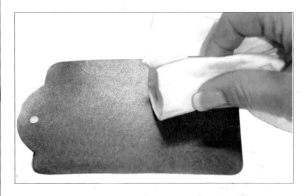

Frosted Embossing

Embossing powder is a beautiful way to make images pop on paper. Because embossing powders are low-melt resins, Perfect Pearls, which have a built-in resin, are attracted to them and will bond to most warm embossing powders.

MATERIALS

- card stock
- Perfect Medium
- embossing powder
- Perfect Pearls
- stamp
- heat gun

Instructions

1 Use the Perfect Medium to stamp an image.

2 Apply embossing powder, shake off the excess, and heat until glossy.

▼

3 Immediately dust with Perfect Pearls to give the embossed image a frosted look.

▼

Radiant Batik

The positive spaces in this paper batik glow. Stamps can be used for this process or designs can be rendered freehand with embossing pens or a Perfect Medium pen.

MATERIALS

- card stock (white or light colored)
- water-based pigments (watercolors, dye inks, water-based markers, etc)
- Perfect Pearls (Gold)
- embossing ink (clear)
- embossing powder (clear)
- paper towel
- stamp
- heat tool
- iron

TIP
▫ Perfect Medium is an all-around craft medium and can be used in place of embossing ink.

Instructions

1 Stamp onto the card stock using embossing ink, then apply powder and heat until glossy.

2 Lightly mist the paper with water and crumble before painting.
▼

3 Mix the water-based pigments with water to form watercolor paints. The intensity of the paints will depend on how much water is added.

4 Paint over the embossing. The spaces where there is no embossing will absorb the paints. If using water-based markers, spray the paper with water and then apply the color.
▼

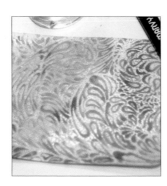

5 Mix Perfect Pearls with water to form a creamy paint and brush over the entire piece. Wipe the paint off the embossing. The embossing is slick, so the paint will wipe off easily but remain on the exposed paper areas.
▼

6 Place the paper (embossing side up) between two pieces of lightweight paper or newsprint and iron on a medium setting. The newsprint will absorb the embossing as it melts off. The paints will set themselves when they are heated.
▼

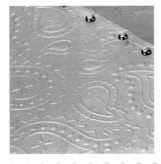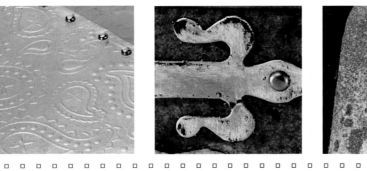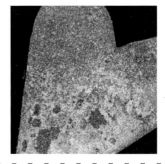

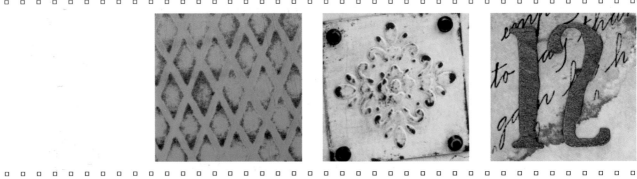

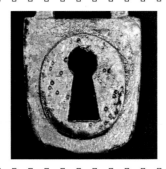

CHAPTER THREE

Metal Look-Alikes

Crafters and artists of all kinds love the look of metal elements. Handles, hinges, and hardware are all popular. It's easy to "fake" these objects using paper, glue, and a few pigments. One of the greatest benefits from making metal-like elements is convenience. They can also be customized in color, size, and shape, and of course—what could be better than feeling like a magician?

The following faux finishes will truly fool the eye and offer great freedom and versatility in the design process. All these finishes are made using paper and a few simple craft supplies, mediums, and adhesives. The results are so much like the real thing it's hard to tell the difference.

Dimension is necessary to create the look of real metal. To achieve this, glue matching elements together until the desired thickness is achieved. Chipboard and illustration board will work, but they can be difficult to cut.

Hammered Copper, Gold, and Silver

The process is the same for all the hammered metals, but the coloring choices differ. Use any paint such as Perfect Pearls, acrylic craft paint, or spray enamels. For a lasting finish use an acrylic medium as a topcoat or a clear acrylic finishing spray. If the piece is for a scrapbook, be certain to use acid-free pigments such as Perfect Pearls and Glossy Accents.

MATERIALS

- die cuts
- adhesive
- Perfect Pearls (Copper, Gold, or Silver)
- brush
- file or sandpaper
- optional: enamel paint, glossy topcoat

Instructions

1 Adhere four to six matching die cuts together.

▼

2 Use a file or a fine grade of sandpaper to smooth the rough edges.

▼

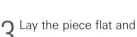

3 Lay the piece flat and use the end of a brush to pound dents into the front surface.

▼

4 Mix Perfect Pearls with water to form a creamy paint and paint the piece, including the sides.

▼

5 For added distressing, lightly sand the edges and surface after the paint is dry.

▼

VARIATION

For a shiny gold or silver, paint with an enamel paint or spray paint, then hammer and distress as before. Apply a glossy topcoat finish.

SUBSTITUTION

Any mica metallic pigment powder can be added to an acrylic paint or medium for this process.

TIP

□ A meat tenderizer can be used to make great pitted surfaces.

Polished Metal

This process is all about chemistry. Embossing powder is a low-melt resin, and when it comes in contact with the resin in Perfect Pearls, a little bonding occurs. Together they create a shining metallic finish.

MATERIALS

■ die cuts

■ adhesive

■ extra-thick embossing powder (clear Ultra Thick Embossing Enamel [UTEE])

■ clear embossing ink

■ Perfect Pearls (metallic)

■ heat tool

Instructions

1 Adhere four to six matching die cuts together.

▶

2 Pat clear embossing ink on top of the piece and liberally sprinkle UTEE embossing powder over the top.

▶

3 Heat until the embossing powder begins to melt and continue to heat while sprinkling on more UTEE. Do this process once or twice to create depth. ▼

4 Allow the piece to cool (but not to become cold) and rub Perfect Pearls into the slightly warm surface. ▶

The powder will bond and make a lovely shiny finish that will last. Allow the piece to completely cool before handling.

Filigree

Filigrees are lacy metal ornaments that have lots of openwork. They are delicate and ornate and add an air of formality and craftsmanship to a project.

MATERIALS

- ■ die cuts
- ■ adhesive
- ■ metallic paint
- ■ optional: glossy acrylic topcoat (clear liquid or spray)

The secret to creating the look of filigree is finding ornate die cuts to work with, or they can be painstakingly hand cut. To create a believable dimension, cut two to four of each piece from card stock. There are many personal die-cut machines and hand punches on the market that will create delicate shapes.

Instructions

1 Adhere two to four matching die cuts together. ▶

2 Paint the piece with any metallic paint. Add a topcoat if desired.

TIPS

- ▫ Add distressing by sanding the edges and stippling patina colors over the piece.
- ▫ Use these pieces to create delicate corners, clock faces, and ornate layered looks.

Hardware

This method is best for flat pieces such as locks, keys, flat hinges, or frames.

MATERIALS

- die cuts
- adhesive
- metallic paints
- sandpaper or file
- optional: sand, embossing powder

Instructions

1 Adhere five to ten matching die cut shapes together. ▼

2 For added dimension, cut and layer more shapes onto the original piece. ▼

3 Use a file or sandpaper to smooth the rough edges. ▼

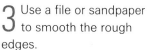

4 Apply a coat of metallic paint.

5 Distress the piece by sanding off some of the paint and pounding dents into the surface.

6 Use patina-colored paints to add more aged effects.

VARIATION

Add more corrosion and texture by adding sand or fine embossing powder to the paint.

Handles and Bent Hinges

This process is all about hardware that's bent and dimensional. This process has to be completed at the time it is started or the glue will dry and the piece can't be manipulated after that.

MATERIALS

 die cuts (AccuCut, photo holders)

■ white glue

■ metallic paints

■ dowel or brush

■ sandpaper or file

Instructions

1 Adhere two or three matching die cuts together.

▼

 While the glue is wet, form the shape around a dowel or brush.

▶

3 When the piece is completely dry, smooth the rough edges.

4 Paint the handle.

TIPS

▫ Try aged effects such as sanding the surface, pounding dents, and adding patina colors.

▫ Be sure to use only two or three layers of die cuts because thinner layers will hold the shape better.

Embossed Tin

Nothing says vintage craftsmanship like embossed tin. Embossed tin pieces were used for ceilings and to adorn everyday objects such as tables and frames. These paper phonies make lovely embellishments for cards and many craft projects.

MATERIALS

- card stock (black)
- paint (silver or pewter)
- brass stencil or texture plate
- embossing stylus or embossing machine
- brush
- sandpaper

Instructions

1 Paint the card stock with the paint and let the piece dry completely before continuing.

▼

2 Emboss the image on the painted card stock.

▶

3 Lightly sand the image to bring out the highlights.

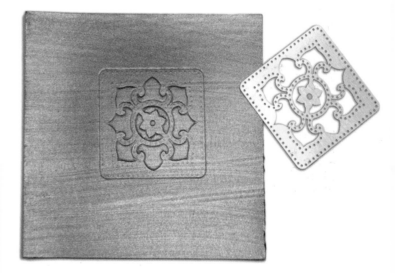

TIPS

- For embossing techniques, see the section on About Embossing (page 84).
- Architectural and graphic designs work best for this effect.

Painted Tin

This is a great technique that can be used to customize the look of embossed metal because it can be painted any color.

MATERIALS

- card stock
- acrylic paint
- brass stencil or texture plate
- embossing stylus or embossing machine
- brush
- sandpaper

Instructions

1 Paint the card stock and allow it to dry completely before continuing.

▼

2 Emboss the image on the painted card stock.

3 Lightly sand the surface to bring out the highlights and added aged effects.

▶

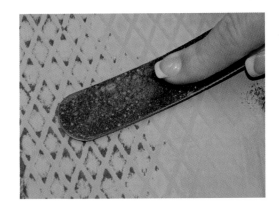

TIPS

- For embossing techniques, see the section on About Embossing (page 84).
- Aged effects can also be put on by dry-brushing paint over the surface.
- To dry-brush, pick up paint on the brush and pounce it on a paper towel to discharge some of the paint, and then paint briskly over the textured surface.

Patina Effects

Patinas are those beautiful corrosive and colorful films that appear on metal and minerals when they have been exposed to the elements or handled often—the mark of something that has endured the forces of nature. Adding patina and aged effects to these faux metal objects adds to their story by implying age, use, or neglect.

MATERIALS

- paper
- paint (patina-like color)
- brush

Patinas form in most every color, but certain metals and minerals have a tendency to grow patina in specific colors. Copper most often corrodes in shades of green, blue, and orange. Iron puts on deep blue and rusty patinas. Brass and bronze turn brown, black, blue, and so on. Choose any colors that seem believable with the project.

Instructions

1 Use any paint with a patina-like color and apply it by stippling. Use one or several colors.

▶

TIP

▫ Perfect Pearls can be added to clear acrylic mediums or mixed with water to form a paint that can be used to create a patina effect.

Corrosive Effects

This method creates the look of super-eroded metal, rust, and grit.

MATERIALS

- paper
- paint (patinalike color)
- acrylic medium
- sand or embossing powder
- brush

Instructions

1 Mix sand or embossing powder in to the patina-colored paint to which an acrylic medium has been added.

▼

2 Paint the surface and stipple on other patina colors if desired.

▼

TIPS

▫ If a spray paint was used, mix sand or embossing powder with an acrylic medium and stipple onto the surface. Paint again and apply any patina color over the top.

▫ Working on sand paper will also create a great corrosive effect.

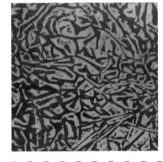

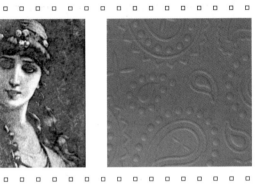

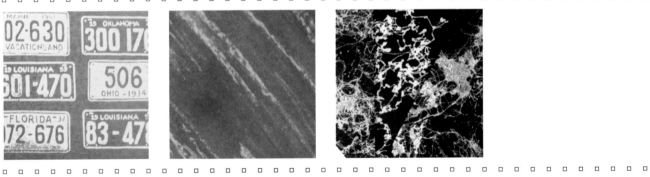

CHAPTER FOUR

Special Paper Treatments

With the advent of new pigments and products, the range of creative possibilities is ever-expanding. Every paper treatment is "special," but there are some that stand apart in uniqueness and process. These treatments include contemporary materials that were not readily available to past artisans. This is a collection of paper processes that will surely spark the creative muse in anyone.

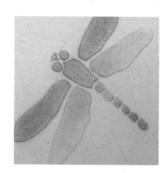

Lifting Color with Bleach

Bleach can be toxic and burn, so be very careful if using it in the craft room. Wear protective clothing, gloves, and safety glasses. Use it in a well-ventilated room. Instead of liquid bleach, which can splash and have strong fumes, use a bleaching pen. The bleach in a laundry pen is a gel and won't splash. It can be squeezed into a small mixing cup for use with a brush or pen.

MATERIALS

- paper
- bleaching laundry pen
- small mixing cup
- eyedropper
- calligraphy pen

TIPS

- Apply heat from a heat tool or an iron to enhance the process.
- Use gel bleach with a brush or sponge for freehand work.

Instructions

1 Squeeze some bleach from the pen into a small mixing cup.

▼

2 Using an eyedropper to avoid splashing, add water to thin the bleach so it will flow from a calligraphy nib and use like any ink.

▼

Lifting Color with Stamps

Bleach is not the best choice for using with rubber stamps because it can damage them. Stamp pad mediums have been developed to lift color. They are easier to use, less toxic, and will not harm stamps like bleach will.

MATERIALS

- paper (dark)
- Castaway Stamp Pad
- stamp (Stamp Oasis, African Background 1234-K)
- brayer
- heat tool

Instructions

1 Press the stamp pad firmly into the stamp.

▼

2 Place the paper onto the stamp and roll the brayer over the paper to transfer the ink to the paper.

▼

3 Apply heat with a heat tool. The color will lighten and alter.

▼

TIPS

- This method does not seem to lift colors as completely as bleach on certain papers, but it still creates contrast and will alter the color.

- If using a smaller stamp, press the stamp firmly into the stamp pad to pick up as much ink as possible and stamp onto the paper.

- An iron or a heat gun are the most common heat tools used with this process.

ABOUT ALCOHOL INK

These vibrant, transparent dye inks come in an alcohol base and do some amazing things when they are layered on to each other. They come in a full range of colors and metallic additives. The beautiful effects of alcohol inks are achieved by applying them to glossy papers or other slick surfaces such as resin dominos, plastic, metal, and even glass. On paper they create the look of polished stones, gems, and shells. Alcohol blending solutions dilute these vibrant inks and are useful as a blending medium. They also clean the inks off surfaces, hands, and tools.

Not all alcohol inks use the same type of alcohol base or pigments, so experiment with the effects before investing heavily in a brand.

Do all these processes on glossy paper. To apply the inks, use cotton squares or balls, cotton swabs, felt, or an alcohol ink applicator.

Tortoiseshell

At one time the only way to get tortoiseshell was from tropical sea turtles, but today there are many synthetic substitutes. This beautiful look of mottled browns and yellows can be re-created on glossy paper with alcohol inks and beautifully mimics the polished look of tortoiseshell.

MATERIALS

- glossy paper
- alcohol inks (black, brown, ochre, or orange)
- alcohol blending solution
- ink applicator

Instructions

1 Drizzle brown ink onto the applicator and lightly pounce all over the paper. ▼

2 Drizzle ochre and black ink onto the same applicator and pounce again all over. The ink will mottle and make patterns. ▼

3 Use a clean applicator and drizzle it with blending solution. Lightly tap the paper in a few places to create faded spots and areas that look more transparent.

Lapis Lazuli

This process is a way to imitate lapis lazuli, a deep-blue mineral that is considered to be a semiprecious gemstone and prized for its rarity.

MATERIALS

- glossy paper
- alcohol inks (brown, gold, three shades of blue)
- alcohol blending solution
- ink applicator
- toothbrush

Instructions

1 Drizzle three shades of blue alcohol inks onto the applicator and pounce over the paper.

2 Allow to dry and repeat the application two more times to create dense color patterns. On the last coat add a small amount of brown to the mix.

3 Put gold alcohol ink on a toothbrush and splatter the surface with fine gold speckles.

Garden Walk

Imagine an aggregated garden walk made from small multicolored stones and naturally polished to a sheen from years of treading. This beautiful paper treatment not only creates the look of many brilliant stones but draws upon nature's garden palette.

MATERIALS

■ glossy paper

■ alcohol inks (ochre, brown, olive, black, terra cotta)

■ alcohol ink blending solution

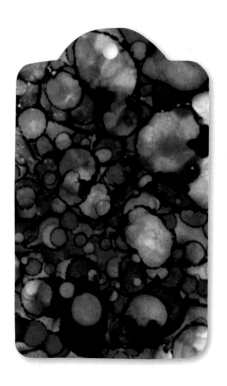

Instructions

1 Do not use an applicator for this treatment. Drip the colors one at a time over the paper finishing with a sprinkle of blending solution.

VARIATION

For a beautiful luminous effect, use a metallic alcohol ink before using the blending solution.

▶

TIP

▫ Try lots of color combinations and methods. For another cool effect, try dripping the blending solution over the paper while manipulating the paper. These inks do all the work and will do something different every time.

ABOUT BEESWAX

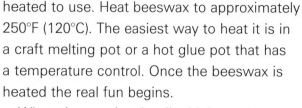

Beeswax has been used for thousands of years as an adhesive and a paint medium. It is combined with resin and pigments to do encaustic, or hot-wax painting (a favorite of the Egyptians). However, beeswax has recently been rediscovered by collage artists and is enjoying a comeback as a fun and funky art medium. Beeswax can be colored, molded, carved, and used as an adhesive. It has a way of melding all the elements of a collage together in its filmy binding.

Beeswax comes in shavings or pellets and must be

heated to use. Heat beeswax to approximately 250°F (120°C). The easiest way to heat it is in a craft melting pot or a hot glue pot that has a temperature control. Once the beeswax is heated the real fun begins.

When the wax is a hot liquid, it can be applied with a brush. Pick a brush that will be used just for hot wax because it won't be good for much else. Beeswax will adhere flat art and dimensional objects. It is quite stable unless it is exposed to extreme heat (higher than 120°F [50°C]).

Beeswax Collage

This is a simple method for using wax to embed collage elements.

MATERIALS

■ paper
■ melted beeswax
■ collage art
■ embellishments
■ brush

Instructions

1 Apply a thin layer of beeswax to the paper and immediately lay the collage art on it.

2 Apply more beeswax over the top to encase the art,

3 This process can be repeated with each element, and multiple layers can be added.

VARIATION

For a luminous beeswax, dry mica powders and Perfect Pearls mica pigments can be added to hot wax. The organic material in these pigments will make the liquid bubble a little, but that is fine. Just be certain not to overheat the wax. Apply this wax over dark paper. The results are dreamy.

TIPS

□ Beeswax cools and hardens very quickly on the paper, so work fast!

□ Drip beeswax over dimensional objects to make them stick.

□ The wax will get cloudier as it becomes thicker with each application.

□ A small amount of oil paint can be added to hot beeswax to make transparent glazes.

□ Dyes with water or alcohol in them will not mix. There are also wax dyes available.

□ Beeswax can be heated with a craft heat tool and manipulated on the paper. It can also be moved around with a wand-type embossing tool or wood burner.

Resist on Glossy Paper

I was teaching a workshop in England once and I asked the participants if they had ever "resisted." After the laughter subsided, we talked about the beauty of images that resist ink to reveal the paper below. Here is an easy method for glossy paper.

MATERIALS

■ glossy paper

■ resist ink

■ dye-based ink

■ paper towel

■ stamp (Post Modern Design, License Plate)

■ brayer

■ optional: spray bottle

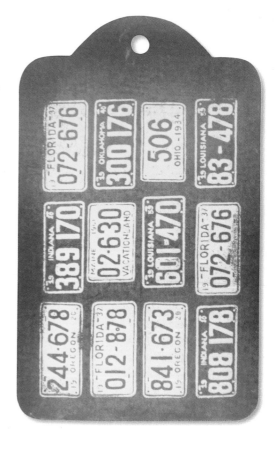

Instructions

1 Ink the stamp with resist ink and stamp onto the glossy paper. Let it dry.
▼

2 Use a brayer to roll the dye-based ink onto the glossy paper over the stamped image.
▼

3 Use a paper towel to remove the excess ink.
▼

TIP

▫ Use a rainbow ink pad with this method to add more visual interest.

VARIATIONS

When the resist image is complete, try adding a mottling effect by spraying clear water over the top, let it rest for a few seconds, and then blot (don't rub) with a paper towel.
▶

To create a resist image other than white, use a brayer to roll dye-based ink onto the paper and use a paper towel to buff off any excess ink. After it dries, follow the instructions above.
▶

SUBSTITUTION

Perfect Medium can work in place of a resist ink.

Heat-Embossed Resist

This is a way to create the look of resisted images on matte paper. The embossing powder acts like a mask by resisting paint and ink during the design process. The embossed image is "melted" off after the piece is finished.

MATERIALS

- paper
- dye-based ink
- clear embossing ink
- clear embossing powder
- paper towel
- stamp (Magenta, 09159.P, and floral)
- brayer
- felt pressing cloth
- iron

Instructions

1 Emboss a clear image onto the paper.

2 Apply the ink with a brayer to reveal the image and wipe off any excess ink with a paper towel.

3 Lay the felt on a table or ironing board, and then place a paper towel on the felt. Lay the image facedown and another paper towel over the paper.

4 Iron with a hot iron until the embossing "melts" off.

TIPS

- For embossing techniques, see the section on About Embossing (page 84).

- The paper can be sprayed with a fine mist of water and rubbed with a paper towel to create a more even application.

- Use a brush with water and the ink to apply color to the details in the image.

Pen Medium Resist

There's nothing better than a process built around personal expressions. Whatever can be done with a pen (writing, drawing, stenciling, designing, journaling, templates, etc) can be done with this resist treatment. An embossing pen or a Perfect Medium pen will work for this process.

MATERIALS

- glossy paper
- embossing pen (Perfect Medium pen)
- dye-based inks
- brayer or sponge

Instructions

1 Write, draw, or stencil on glossy paper with the embossing or Perfect Medium pen.

▶

2 Use a brayer or sponge to apply dye-based ink over the embossed image.

▶

Crayon or Wax Pencil Resist

A quick and easy way to lay down a resist on matte paper is to use a wax-based material in stick form.

MATERIALS

- paper
- dye-based ink
- crayon or wax pencil
- optional: watercolor, Perfect Pearls

Instructions

1 Write, draw, or stencil on paper with the crayon or wax pencil. ▼

2 Use a brayer or sponge to apply dye-based ink over the crayon or wax pencil. ▼

VARIATION

Use a luminous watercolor or mix a small amount of Perfect Pearls with water to form a thin paint to brush over the crayon or wax pencil. ▼

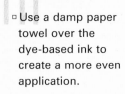

TIP
▫ Use a damp paper towel over the dye-based ink to create a more even application.

Wax Paper Batik

This is a great method for replicating those delicate fractured lines that occur on batik-dyed fabric. This process works on most paper (matte or glossy) and vellum. Wax paper can be hard to find sometimes, but most restaurant supply retailers have it and some grocery stores still carry it. It is wonderful to have around the arts and crafts room.

MATERIALS

- paper
- scrap paper
- dye-based inks
- wax paper
- paper towel
- felt pressing cloth
- iron

Instructions

1 Take the wax paper and crumple it repeatedly until the desired texture is achieved.

2 Lay the felt on a table or ironing board, and then place the scrap paper on the felt. Lay the crumpled wax paper on the scrap paper and place the paper for printing on top of the wax paper. ▼

3 Iron with a hot iron. ▼

4 After the paper cools, apply the ink to reveal the pattern and wipe off any excess ink. ▼

Try folding the wax paper to create lines and geometric effects.

▶

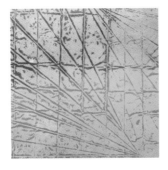

Create the batik in a shape by taking crumpled wax paper and punching or die-cutting shapes from it before ironing.

▼

Cut snowflakes or other mirrored-imaged shapes from folded wax paper, then iron.

▶

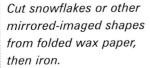

Solvent Pen Transfers

There is something mysterious about an image that is barely there. It makes a person wonder about its history, age, and who may have handled it over time. There are many ways to transfer images to paper, many of which re-create pristine images, but there is nothing like a hand-worked image transfer. It takes on the look of aged and used paint or ink and immediately speaks of the artist's touch. This process is quite simple with good results, but be sure to do it in a well-ventilated room because the chemical has strong fumes.

MATERIALS

- smooth surface paper
- photocopy of the image to be transferred
- paper towel or bone folder
- blending pen (Chartpak Blender)
- removable tape or paper clip

Instructions

1 Reverse the image of the photo to be transferred and make a copy. Cut out the image to be transferred, leaving a 1" (2.5 cm) border all around.

▶

2 Lay the image face-down on the paper and secure it with removable tape or a paper clip.

3 Apply the solvent to the back of the image with the blender pen.

▶

4 Burnish the image firmly on the back with a paper towel or a bone folder. Repeat the process if needed.

▼

5 Remove the top image to reveal the faded image beneath.

▼

TIPS

□ This process will work with images produced on some ink-jet printers, so test the process first to see if it works. This process always works with color copies using a toner-based ink.

□ The Chartpak Blender is different from the blender pens that come with water-based markers. It is a solvent-based pen.

ABOUT DRY EMBOSSING

Embossing is any process that raises an image from the paper surface. Artists and crafters have discovered the beauty of these images that seem to be trying to escape the paper. Thankfully, there are many tools and mediums that make the embossing process quick and easy. There are embossing powders, pastes, and paints that can create raised images. Dry embossing uses only paper, a template, and pressure from a stylus or machine. Embossing is another ancient process, and beautifully embossed papers are considered art treasures by collectors.

Dry Embossing by Hand

There are several types of styluses to use for hand embossing. The traditional tool has a wooden handle with a metal ball on one or both ends. There are also styluses that have a rolling ball mechanism. Both come in different sizes and work with most stencils. A light box is used with light-colored papers whereas dark-colored papers pose a challenge because the light from the light box does not show through them. Therefore, a different method is used for embossing on dark papers.

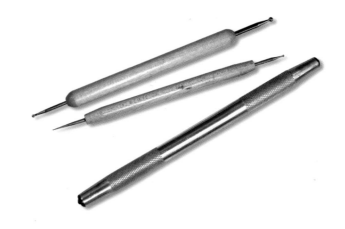

MATERIALS

- ■ paper
- ■ embossing stencil
- ■ stylus
- ■ light box or foam mat
- ■ removable tape

Instructions for Embossing on Light-Colored Paper

1 Lay the stencil on the light box and turn it on. Lay the paper over the stencil and use removable tape to keep them secure.

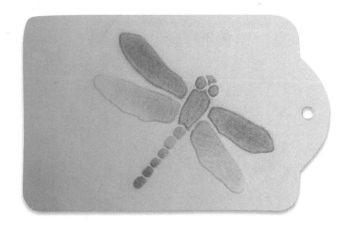

2 Use a stylus to emboss by gently pressing down into the open parts of the stencil, which will be illuminated by the light. ▶

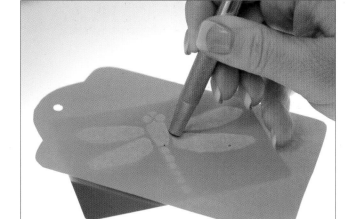

Instructions for Embossing on Dark-Colored Paper

1 Use removable tape to secure the stencil to the paper. Lay the paper and stencil with the stencil side up on a foam embossing mat and use a stylus to score an outline of the areas to be embossed. ▶

2 Turn the paper over and use the scoring lines as guides and continue embossing. ▶

Dry Embossing by Machine

Anyone that has ever wanted to make thirty matching cards or invitations with embossed elements knows it's going to take some time to produce them using the "old-fashioned" hand embossing method. Fortunately, there are now personal die-cut machines, most of which have embossing capabilities. These machines not only cut beautiful die cuts, but they can emboss in an instant. Some have their own embossing stencils and texture plates. It is so wonderful to produce these elements in just a few seconds. These machines also make it easy to make larger pieces of embossed paper, which means they can be used on bigger scale projects. Shop around to find the right machine.

MATERIALS

- paper
- embossing stencil or texture plate
- personal die-cut machine with embossing capabilities
- optional: glossy acrylic medium

Instructions

1 Follow the instructions that come with the machine. Every machine has its own process.

Some embossing machines will emboss actual objects if the objects aren't too thick to go through the machine. ▼ ▶

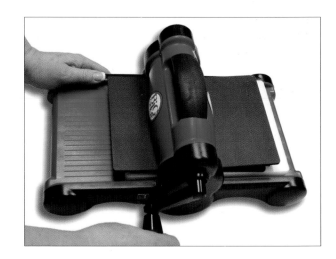

VARIATION

To create the look of patent leather, glaze paper with a glossy acrylic medium and allow it to dry before embossing.

▶

TIPS

▫ To color embossed ▶ images, leave the stencil in place after embossing and use inks or chalks on the exposed paper parts. The stencil will act like a mask; just remove it when finished.

▫ Try embossing painted papers and then sanding lightly to create aged effects. This looks great if the paper is dark and the paint is light.

▫ For card stock and extra-thick paper, mist them lightly and quickly wipe off the water with

a paper towel, then emboss. The moisture will keep the paper from fracturing during the process.

▫ Rubbing the hand stylus on wax paper every now and then helps it glide easier.

Spray Webbing

Cobwebs can be beautiful (minus their landlords), sparkling with dew or silhouetted against a contrasting background. Reproducing those intricate connected threads of color makes a lovely visual statement. One of the simplest ways to produce webbing is to purchase a webbing spray paint that has a special nozzle designed to produce webbed effects. The nice thing about webbing sprays is that the paint is tacky for a moment after it hits the paper and some additional treatments can be added.

MATERIALS

■ paper

■ webbing spray paint

Instructions

1 The can will have instructions, but just aim and spray!

VARIATION

For foiled webbing, immediately place a metallic leafing sheet over the piece and gently burnish off the excess foil with a soft brush.

TIP

▫ While the paint is wet, dust with Perfect Pearls Interference colors for a two-tone effect.

▫ The farther the can is held from the paper, the more open and airy the design; spraying too close can make clumps.

Metallic Leafing

There is no better way to add a touch of extravagance than by using metallic leafing. Metallic leafing can be found in a rainbow of colors, but gold and silver are the most popular. From sheets to flakes, leafing comes in a variety of forms.

MATERIALS

- paper
- ink
- stamp
- leafing size
- metallic leafing
- brush
- soft wide brush
- optional: calligraphy pen

Instructions

1 Stamp the image using the ink and let it dry.
▼

2 Apply the leafing size to anywhere on the image.
▼

3 Place the metallic leaf over the leafing size and press down with the soft brush. Lightly burnish away any excess leafing.
▼

VARIATION

Dilute the leafing size with water to use in a calligraphy pen. Use two parts leafing size and one part water. Write your design, then apply the leaf.
▶

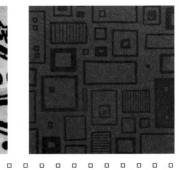

CHAPTER FIVE

Stamping Techniques

Before printing presses and copy machines there were stamps. Stamps are the most basic of printmaking tools—and they're fun and easy to use. It would be impossible to discuss transforming paper without mentioning stamps and some of the imaginative stamping processes that are used to create breathtaking papers. Artists and crafters seem as drawn to these processes as they are to the imagery.

ABOUT STAMPING INKS ▫ ▫ ▫ ▫ ▫ ▫ ▫ ▫ ▫ ▫ ▫ ▫ ▫ ▫ ▫ ▫ ▫

Stamps can be made from rubber, polymer, foam, sponge, metal, wood, linoleum, or a potato from the refrigerator. They come unmounted or mounted on wood and acrylic blocks. They come in the shape of wheels, mats, on the ends of dowels, and so on. No wonder stamps have caught the fancy of artists—they radiate with diversity and creativity. Just to hold a stamp is to be filled with inspiration.

There are many stamp inks available and it would be near impossible to name all the brands and their differences. The following is a list of ink types and their most common uses.

PIGMENT INK

These inks are pigment-based, slow drying, and slightly tacky so they are the ink to **use with embossing powders.** They can also be blended on matte paper to create some great background effects. They are **not for glossy paper,** unless they are embossed, because they don't dry.

DYE-BASED INK

These water-based inks are more like watercolors and transparent dyes. They come in ink pads, liquid re-inkers, sprays, and markers. Dye-based inks are faster drying and can be used to create washy watercolor effects as well as pristine stamped images. **They cannot be used for embossing.**

SOLVENT-BASED INK

Solvent inks were developed for **nonporous surfaces such as glass, metal, glossy papers, or plastic.** They come in transparent versions, which are less toxic than the opaque versions.

They are available in stamp pads, paints, and markers. Solvent cleaners are available with these inks.

CHALK INKS

These inks have a pigment base, but they are opaque and dry to a **very matte, powdery finish.** They are great because they show up on dark papers.

RAINBOW STAMPING PADS

These pads come with several colors all in one pad. They are fun because stamped images appear **multicolored.** They are available in water-based and pigment ink collections.

METALLIC AND MICA STAMPING PADS

These pads are usually pigment-based and are designed to give a **luminous quality to stamped images.** Some are made to dry faster, which makes them more versatile.

HEAT-SET INKS

Heat setting makes these **pigments more permanent and the colors more vibrant.** They are great to use on almost any surface, including slick surfaces and fabric.

ARCHIVAL INK

These inks are water-based and are designed to resist water when they are dry. The **colors are vibrant and should last many years to come.** They are, of course, acid-free and archival safe.

THE NEWBIES

There is a whole new family of inks that don't exactly match the other types. They can be used to emboss and yet they dry quickly so they can be used like dye inks as well. Some have a light solvent base and some are pigment based.

CASTAWAY STAMP PAD

This is called ink because it comes in a stamp pad, but this pad actually lifts or alters the original color of the paper when heat is applied. It creates some very interesting tone-on-tone effects.

Most ink manufacturers make information about their products easily accessible on the packaging or online.

ABOUT EMBOSSING POWDER

Embossing powders are low-melt resins that come in granules. They melt when they are heated with a heat tool, but get hard again when they cool. They can be used to make stamped images pop or to make interesting dimensional effects.

DETAIL OR FINE EMBOSSING POWDER

These powders are the finest in texture and should be used to emboss images that have a lot of fine detail.

REGULAR EMBOSSING POWDER

This is the most all-purpose powder and is good for embossing most stamp images.

EXTRA-THICK EMBOSSING POWDER

This is a grainy embossing powder that is used for special effects. It can also be used to emboss very bold stamp images, but fine details will be lost. This type of embossing powder can be heated in a melting pot and poured into molds to make custom embellishments.

DISTRESS EMBOSSING POWDERS

These powders have a release crystal in them that doesn't bond to the paper so after the embossing powder is heated some of it can be rubbed off to create the look of peeled paint and rusty metal.

SPECIALTY EMBOSSING POWDERS

There are many other embossing powders that have specific looks and do specific tasks, which include pearls, metallics, tinsels, sparkles and glitters, flocks, and many custom colors and collections.

EMBOSSING ADHESIVE

This embossing power is actually an adhesive that becomes tacky when heated. It will adhere to foils, metallic leaf, and a variety of pigments.

Basic Heat Embossing

Embossing powder is heated with a heat tool. There are several styles of heat tools. One is long and has a nozzle at the end that blows hot air. Another looks like a small blowdryer and the heat is more diffused, which keeps the embossing powder from blowing away. There are good uses for both types.

MATERIALS

- paper
- pigment ink
- embossing powder
- stamp
- heat tool

Instructions

1 Stamp the image using pigment ink.

2 Sprinkle embossing powder over the image, holding the paper vertically over a collecting tray or scrap paper to catch the excess powder as it falls off. Return the excess power to the container.

3 Apply heat until the powder melts.

TIPS

- Don't overheat the powder or it will burn off.
- Lightly brush the paper with cornstarch to help keep the embossing powder from clinging to unwanted areas.

Extra-Thick Embossing

These thick powders make great special effects on paper. They can look like glass or tiles and are great to stamp on or into. They are also good for making aged effects. They come in clear, metallic, and colored versions.

MATERIALS

- card stock or illustration board
- embossing ink (clear)
- extra-thick embossing powder (gold)
- stamp
- heat tool

Instructions

1 Tap the stamp into the embossing ink and set aside. This will help the stamp release later.

2 Trim a piece of card stock or illustration board to the desired size and pat with embossing ink.
▼

3 Sprinkle the card stock or illustration board with embossing powder. Shake off the excess powder and heat the piece with a heat tool.
▼

4 Keep the heat on the piece and sprinkle more powder over the top. It will melt into the first

layer and create more dimension. This process can be repeated.
▼

5 While the embossing powder is still molten, press the stamp into it. Allow the embossing to cool before removing the stamp.
▼

TIP

▫ The image can be enhanced by rubbing it with inks or Perfect Pearls to bring out the highlights.

Stamped Watercolor Effects

It is always amazing how watercolors appear to just flow onto the page and mysteriously gather to form images. This stamp method produces miniature watercolor paintings that are so lovely they deserve a frame.

MATERIALS

- card stock or very fine-tooth watercolor paper
- dye-based ink
- stamp (JudiKins, 2558 H)
- fine-mist spray bottle

Instructions

1 Press the stamp firmly into the ink.

▼

2 Spray the stamp with water. The ink will start to bead on the stamp.

▼

3 Stamp the image onto the paper.

TIPS

- The stamp can be sprayed with water again and the image stamped onto paper up to three times.

▼

- Water-based inks are the only type of inks that work for this method.
- Choose an image with bold detail; fine details will be lost.

Watermarking

Watermarks are faint images that appear on paper. There are watermark inks that create this look. The inks are clear but they deepen the tones on the paper and make subtle changes. Perfect Medium, which is a stamp medium, also makes beautiful crisp watermarks.

MATERIALS

- card stock (dark colored)
- watermark ink
- stamp

Instructions

1 Stamp the image using watermark ink. All done!

▶

Soot Prints

Stamping into soot creates the unique look of aged negatives or old prints. The secret to creating this look is to deposit soot on glossy paper and then lifting it off with a stamp to reveal the image. Because the soot is dark in color, it creates a negative effect. It is necessary to apply a topcoat to preserve the image. Picking the right stamp is important to this method, so choose stamps with clear images and not too much fine detail.

MATERIALS

- glossy card stock
- acrylic topcoat spray (clear)
- candle
- stamp
- optional: dye-based ink

Instructions

1 Place the candle in a holder and light it.

2 Hold the paper 1" to 2" (2.5–5.0 cm) away from the flame and ▶ tilt the paper so the soot collects on the paper surface.
▼

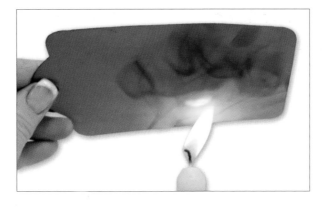

VARIATION

To create more colorful images, apply dye ink to the paper with a sponge or brayer before creating soot on the surface. When this paper is stamped, it will reveal the colored ink beneath.

3 Stamp on the soot-covered paper.
▼

4 Spray with a topcoat so the soot and image will not rub off.

TIP

□ Try coating the paper with sepia or straw-colored ink for more vintage-looking prints.

Overstamping and Layering

Stamping over just about any of these paper treatments makes a great statement. Stamping over stamping is also a great technique. Layering multiple techniques creates amazing depth and interest. This is a great way to let the imagination run wild and become a mad inventor. It is so much fun mixing techniques, and the results are impressive and personal. The following sample uses five different methods and a few aging techniques.

MATERIALS

- paper and card stock
- die cuts
- dye-based inks
- stamps
- gold leafing
- leafing size
- paper towel
- spray bottle
- soft brush

Instructions

1 Using dye-based inks, apply them to the tag using a direct-to-paper technique. ▼

2 Mottle the paper by spraying droplets over it and blotting it with a paper towel. ▼

3 Stamp the first image. ▼

4 Find a place on the image to apply leafing size, paint it on, and then apply the gold leaf. ▼

5 Burnish off the extra leaf with a soft brush.

6 Stamp over the entire tag with a crackle image stamp. ▼

7 Rip a small corner off the tag.

8 Add aging to the edges of the tag with dye-based ink.

9 Embellish with a Roman coin, made by layering four card stock discs, inking the top, and stamping the image.

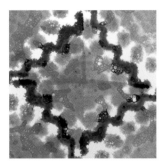

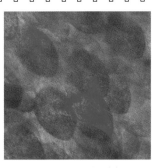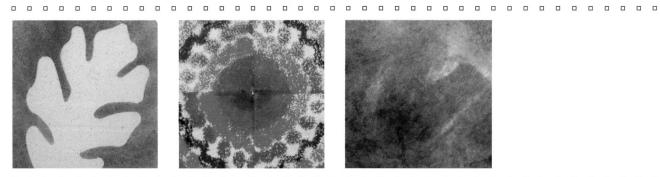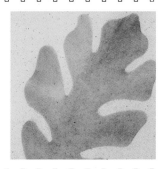

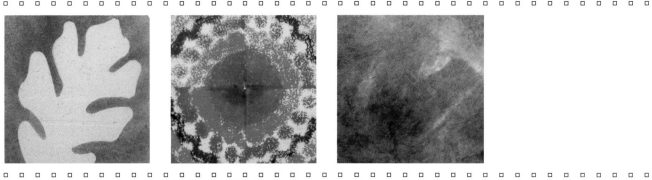

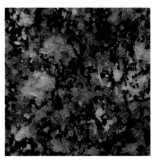

CHAPTER SIX

Stippling, Sponging, and Stenciling

The age-old techniques of the three S's have never lost their appeal to the paper artist. These techniques are a quick and easy way to add color and design to paper. Textures and images can be effortlessly added to paper in layers to create striking depth. It is easy to be deeply engaged with the three S's and it will be hard to know when to stop.

Stippling Methods

Stippling is a form of applying ink by pouncing the brush up and down on the paper. You can do this with any brush, but an actual stippling brush is best because the hairs are stiff and create an airbrushed effect. Stippling can be used to add shading and to define images. Use this technique with stencils and templates for defined images.

MATERIALS

- paper or card stock
- ink or paint
- stipple brush

Instructions

1 Apply ink or paint directly to paper using a dry stipple brush.

▶

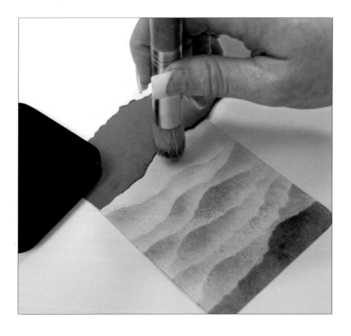

TIPS

- Load the brush sparingly when using paint. Discharge extra paint onto a paper towel before applying it to the paper.

- Use stencils, die cuts, or torn paper to create patterns or shapes.

Direct-to-Paper Techniques

In this process, ink is applied directly to the paper from the ink pad or ink applicator. There are also styluses that have a variety of shaped sponge applicators just for this process.

MATERIALS

- paper or card stock
- ink (pigment or dye-based)
- optional: ink applicator, paper towel

Instructions

1 Start with the lightest shade of color and apply by tapping or dragging the ink pad directly on the paper.

▼

2 Continue the process of layering the colors, working from light to dark.

▼

3 Use a paper towel to buff and blend the effects if desired.

▼

TIP

▫ The process is the same using the stylus tool, only the inks are deposited in patterns and shapes.

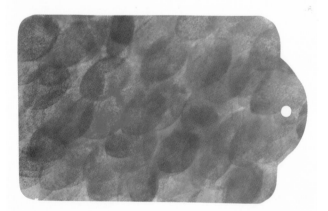

Compressed Sponge Designing

Compressed sponges are unique sponges that absorb inks in a controlled area and can be used to create patterns, stripes, and special effects.

MATERIALS

- card stock (matte or glossy)
- dye inks (Posh Inkabililties)
- compressed sponge

Instructions for Patterns

1 Draw an image in ink on the flat surface of the sponge and stamp the image onto paper.

▶

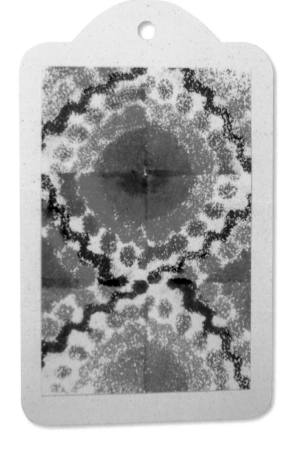

2 The sponge can be turned and manipu-lated in different directions ▼

to make different patterns from the same inked sponge. ▼

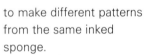

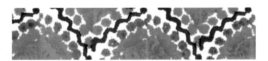

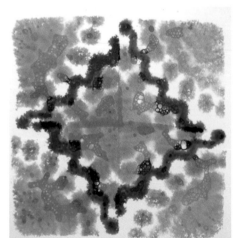

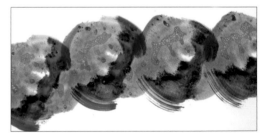

Instructions for Stripes

1 Apply the inks on the ridge of the sponge.

▼

2 Drag the sponge across the paper.

▼

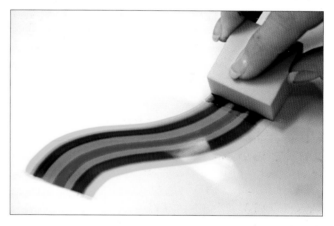

TIPS

▫ The design will get lighter with each use. You can mist the sponge with water to revive the color.

▫ Matte paper will absorb more ink than glossy paper.

Sea Sponge Techniques

Natural sea sponges have been used for centuries as art tools for making wonderful paint effects. No two sponges are alike so every design will be unique. There is something wonderfully organic about this process and it is a real hands-on type of painting.

MATERIALS

- paper or card stock
- paints or inks
- sea sponge
- spray bottle
- optional: metallic paints, Perfect Pearls

Natural sea sponges can be expensive, but synthetic sea sponges are very inexpensive. The synthetic sponges have more of a uniform pattern whereas every natural sea sponge is a work of nature.

Instructions

1 Spray the sponge with water to soften.

2 Thin paints with water if need. Sponge paints onto the paper, layering light and dark colors.

▶

VARIATION

Use metallic paints or create your own metallic paints with Perfect Pearls to make a luminous sponging effect.

▶

Negative and Positive Stenciling

There are two basic ways to use a stencil. The positive image, the actual shape, looks and acts very much like a die cut. The negative image is the more traditional stencil where the shape is an empty space.

When placed onto the paper, the positive stencil produces a negative image on the paper. Likewise, when the negative stencil is used, it produces a positive image on the paper.

MATERIALS

- paper or card stock
- pigments (inks, paint, pastels, etc)
- applicator
- stencil

Instructions for Positive Stenciling

1 Place a positive stencil on the paper or card stock.

2 Apply the pigments around the stencil to the paper.

▼

Instructions for Negative Stenciling

1 Place a negative stencil over the paper or card stock.

2 Apply the pigments on the exposed parts of the paper.

▼

TIPS

□ Use a low-tack adhesive to keep stencils in place.

□ Some pigments may require a fixative when finished.

Stenciling with Punched Images

Die cuts and punches are a great way to create customized stencils.

MATERIALS

■ paper or card stock

■ pigments (inks, paint, pastels, etc)

■ applicator

■ paper punch

Instructions

1 Create the stenciling shape from card stock.

2 Place the stencil over the paper or card stock.

3 Apply the pigments on the exposed parts of the paper.

▶

TIP

▫ This is a great way to make customized borders.

Overstenciling

There is something intriguing about a negative and positive image together. They make a very bold and graphic statement and the contrast is a declaration by itself.

MATERIALS

■ paper or card stock

■ pigments (inks, paint, pastels, etc)

■ applicator

■ stencil

Instructions

1 Place a negative or positive stencil over the paper or card stock.

2 Apply the pigments.

3 Repeat the steps, switching the positive and negative stencils.

VARIATION

Use only a negative stencil with color-lifting techniques and inks to create the illusion of negative and positive.

   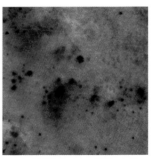

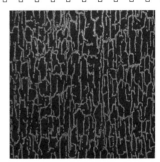

CHAPTER SEVEN

Paper Finales

This chapter covers paper finishes, the final step in a project that is often responsible for the tone and mood of a piece. Finishes include glazes and topcoats. Technically, a glaze is a shiny finish, but a topcoat can be one of several finishing treatments. There are three distinct finishing options: matte, satin, and gloss. A clear matte finish is flat and can be hard to see on a surface. It is there to protect the artwork without contributing design function. A satin finish is not totally flat and adds a small amount of luster to the surface. A glossy finish is the shiniest and can have a mirrorlike reflection.

ABOUT FINISHING

There are excellent choices in finishing treatments for paper, including acrylic mediums, to which any water-based pigments can be added, as well as water-based paints and inks. Acrylic mediums can have thin, regular, or gel-like consistencies.

Dyes and stains can be finishes if they contribute to the overall appearance of a piece.

The following examples were all given a walnut ink topcoat, but each was done in a different hue.

After

Before

Luminous finishes, such as dry mica-based pigment powders, can be added to any acrylic medium to form a water-resistant topcoat. Mica dry pigment powders can also be added to gum arabic, but this will not be a water-resistant finish. Perfect Pearls have built-in resins and binders and create beautiful luminous finishes when mixed with water.

There are stamps that can be used to create the look of surfaces and topcoats such as crackle finishes, wood grains, sponging, linen, and so on. These come in handy for quick finishing treatments.

Interference Color Finishes

At first glance, interference colors may look bland and colorless, but when applied to projects they pack a wallop. The light color is due to the transparent nature of the luminous base in these special pigments. They can be used to create beautiful transparent paints and glazes.

MATERIALS

- paper (black or dark colored)
- Perfect Pearls (Interference)
- paper towel
- brush
- optional: photograph

Instructions

1 Mix Perfect Pearls with water to form a creamy paint.

2 Apply the paint in both directions on the paper and buff gently with a paper towel.

VARIATION

Apply the paint over a photograph for luminous tinting.

TIP

- If using another powder mica pigment, mix with an acrylic medium.

ABOUT AGING TECHNIQUES

There is something romantic and wistful about objects that look aged and worn. We value these things and call them such names as "vintage," "antiques," "keepsakes," and "heirlooms." They are objects to be cherished.

This may be why so many artists incorporate aged effects in their works, perhaps in the hopes of capturing that special feeling of an object that has clearly experienced life.

Hammering

Another artist made me a tool that has become an absolute favorite of mine. He took a rubber hammer and inserted linoleum nails from the hardware store into one end. I use this customized hammer to pound indents into all kind of things, including faux hardware.

MATERIALS

- paper
- fine-mist spray bottle
- customized hammer or brush
- foam (mouse pad or foam embossing mat)
- iron

Instructions

1 Lightly mist the paper and wipe it off. This will keep the paper from fracturing during the pounding process.

2 Use the hammer or the back of a brush to lightly pound indents into the paper.

3 Iron the paper flat from the side that was pounded on.

Sanding

When an object has been handled a lot, its edges often lose their paint and luster. This is the look sanding can create. Sanding creates the best effects when there is a contrast in color to show where the sanding occurred.

MATERIALS

- ■ card stock (dark colored)
- ■ pigments (ink, paint, chalk, etc)
- ■ sandpaper (the grade depends upon the desired effect)

Instructions

1 Apply a paper treatment (painted, inked, chalked, etc) that is lighter in color than the paper.

2 Sand the edges and high points of the pieces to create contrast and worn effects.

TIP

□ This is a great technique to use with embossed pieces that have been painted.

ABOUT DYEING AND STAINING

Aged paper is often discolored and stained. An easy way to reproduce these looks is by using transparent antiquing pigments such as tea stains, walnut inks, and distressing inks.

For an interesting effect, try folding, crumpling, and creasing the paper before staining. The fractures in the paper will pick up more color.

Allow the paper to dry completely and try adding more layers of stain.

Tea Dyeing

Turning fabrics and paper off-white was a challenge in days past. A popular process was to boil fabrics with tea, which stained the fabric permanently. Paper can also be tea stained to create soft muted colors.

MATERIALS

- tea bags (six to ten)
- boiling water (2 cups [250 ml])
- paper
- brush
- optional: iron, heat tool

Instructions

1 Place the tea bags in boiling water and allow them to steep until the water naturally cools to room temperature. Remove the tea bags before using the dye.

2 Brush the dye over the paper and allow it to dry. A warm iron or a heat tool can be used to speed up the drying. This process can be repeated several times.

TIP

Add fruit juice to the tea to create more color variations. Some good juices are cherry, grape, blueberry, and cranberry.

Walnut Inks

Walnut inks are transparent stains that are actually made from walnut shell bases. They come in liquid form, sprays, and as crystals. Walnut inks are masters at making paper appear old and damaged, and they are a very stable, long-lasting pigment.

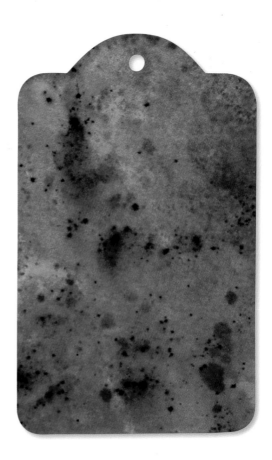

MATERIALS

- walnut ink
- paper
- brush

Instructions

1 Apply the ink to the paper. Use a brush to apply ink in specific areas so it will create puddle effects. Allow the paper to dry naturally.

VARIATION

Use the walnut granules in solid form by sprinkling them over wet paper.

▶

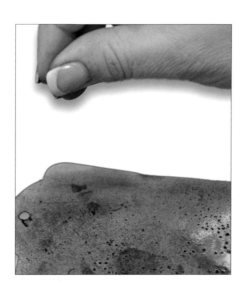

TIP

There are many inks available that will create the look of age and wear on paper, similar to the effects of walnut ink. The most important thing is to choose colors that reflect the era and age desired. There are colors that replicate tea dye, walnut inks, and sepia pigments.

Charring

There is something so intriguing about a piece of paper that was clearly once in danger of being destroyed. Burned and charred paper implies a survivor's story, which makes the piece more of a treasure.

MATERIALS

■ paper
■ ink
■ stamp
■ candle

Instructions

1 Stamp the image onto the paper.

2 Light the candle and carefully char the edges and/or face of the paper piece. Use a damp sponge or a bowl of water to douse the flames.

TIP

▫ Be careful doing this technique. It's easy to start a little fire, so keep a spray bottle of water close by.

Tearing and Fraying

Nothing says tattered and aged like rips and tears. Part of the beauty of working with paper is that it is not difficult to tear, so incorporating these kinds of special effects is easy.

MATERIALS

■ paper or card stock

Instructions

1 Tear and rip the paper.

TIPS

▫ Try layering torn pieces and applying ink to the edges for added definition.

▫ A torn paper edge will be different with one side being smoother than the other. Different types of edges are created depending on if the paper is torn in a forward direction or a backwards one.

▫ Rulers with deckled edges have been developed to make tearing decorative edges a breeze.

Peeled Paint

Shabby chic is always in style; barn doors, painted antiques, weathered shutters, and wooden swings are just a few of the images that peeling paint brings to mind. This fun process creates the look of chipped paint on paper. Use it to make boxes look like painted wooden treasures, plaques, altered art, and so on. This is one fun paper!

MATERIALS

- chipboard or illustration board
- acrylic paint (two contrasting colors)
- petroleum jelly
- paper towel
- brush

Instructions

1 Paint the paper with the color that is to be peeking through the chipped areas. Let it dry completely before continuing.

▶

2 Apply petroleum jelly randomly over the painted paper.

▶

3 Paint the second color over the paper with long even strokes. Try to work the paint as little as possible so the petroleum jelly doesn't blend. Let this dry until the paper can be touched without smearing.
▶

4 Take a paper towel and rub off areas of the paint.
▶

White Glue Crackle

Crackled finishes are a sure sign of age and they only happen naturally over time, but this process takes moments with no special supplies.

MATERIALS

- card stock (choose a paper that is the desired undertone color)
- white glue (real school glue, not a white acrylic)
- acrylic paint
- brush

Instructions

1 Paint the paper with a thin application of white glue and let it dry until it is tacky, but not dry.

▶

2 Paint the paper over the glue with acrylic paint and let this dry naturally to reveal the crackles.

▶

TIP

□ To create fine lines and crackles, keep the paint thick. For wider cracks, thin the paint with water.

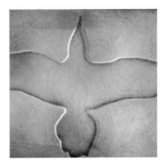

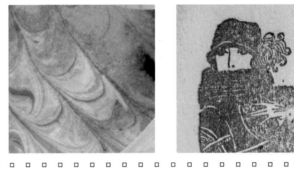

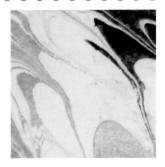

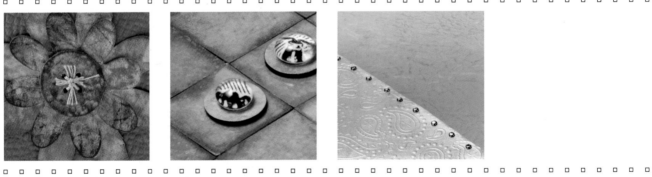

CHAPTER EIGHT

Sparkling Paper Projects

Marbled Asian Coin Card

RECIPES AND TECHNIQUES

Basic Water Marbling, Metallic Leafing

MATERIALS

- water-marbled rice paper
- card stock (coral, cream)
- tissue paper
- embellishments (Asian coin, small tassel)
- gold leaf (La D'ore)
- leafing size (La D'ore)
- adhesive
- brush

Instructions

1 Make a 6" × 6" (15.2 × 15.2 cm) card from coral card stock.

2 Trim the cream card stock to 4¼" × 5¾" (10.8 × 14.6 cm) and adhere it to the front of the card.

3 Trim the water marbled paper to 4" × 5½" (10.2 × 14 cm) and adhere it to the coral card.

4 Apply the gold leaf in a 1" (2.5 cm) square in the center of a 3" (7.6 cm) square piece of tissue paper.

5 Adhere the tissue paper to the water marbled paper.

6 Adhere the coin to the center of the gold leaf.

7 Tie the tassel to the folded edge of the card.

This card features a lovely background of watercolor marbling on traditional rice paper. A small square of tissue paper showcases a gold leaf square and an authentic Asian coin.

Beeswax Button Box

RECIPES AND TECHNIQUES

Resist on Glossy Paper, Mottled Paper, Overstamping, Paper-to-Paper Image Transfer, Beeswax

MATERIALS

- glossy and matte card stock (white)
- box
- clear beeswax
- photocopy of the image to be transferred
- solvent blender pen
- dye-based inks
- permanent ink
- resist ink or Perfect Medium
- embellishments (buttons, ribbon)
- adhesive
- paper towels
- stamps (Magenta, 19008-I; Postmodern Design, AR3-104-D; Stampers Anonymous, J1-664, K222, M3-654; Stamp Francisco, Carpe Diem)
- brush
- spray bottle

Instructions

1 Apply ink to the box and mottle with water.

2 Cut four glossy card stock panels ¼" (6 mm) smaller than the actual sides of the box.

3 Stamp on the panels using resist ink, and sponge the dye-based ink over the top. Buff off the excess ink with a paper towel.

4 Mottle the panels.

5 Overstamp the panels with permanent ink.

6 Cut a lid panel from the matte card stock. Reverse the image of the photo to be transferred and make a copy. Transfer the copied image to the lid panel using the solvent pen.

7 Glue the panels in place and brush with hot beeswax.

8 Drip the wax in to a puddle and attach the buttons. Tie the box with a ribbon.

A box is covered with
beautiful decorative panels.
An angelic cherub image is
transferred to the box's top
and adorned with buttons.
The entire piece is coated
in beeswax to create a soft,
milky sheen.

Bleached Holiday Card

RECIPES AND TECHNIQUES

Lifting Color with Bleach, Heat Embossing, Watercolor Pencils

MATERIALS

- card stock (blue, cream, red, white)
- watercolor pencils
- bleach pen
- embossing ink
- embossing powder (black)
- embellishments (brads, red ribbon)
- adhesive
- stamp (Magenta, 02180-L)
- heat tool
- brush

Instructions

1 Make the snowflake pattern on the blue card stock by drawing polka dots with a bleach pen.

2 Trim the snowflake paper to 5⅜" (13.7 cm) square and mat with cream card stock.

3 Tie a red ribbon around the left side and adhere this piece to a 6" (15.2 cm) square red card.

4 Stamp the image on white card stock and emboss with black embossing powder. Color the image with watercolor pencils and use water to turn it to paint.

5 Trim the image to 3" (7.6 cm) square and mat with red and cream card stock. Attach the brads at the corners and then attach it to the center of the snowflake paper.

On this card, a playful holiday image is hand-colored with watercolor pencils. The delightful snowflake paper that frames the center image is created by lifting color with a bleach pen.

Embossed Wall Vase

RECIPES AND TECHNIQUES

Embossed Tin, Hammered Metal

MATERIALS

- papier-mâché (JuliaAndrus.com, wall vase)
- card stock (black)
- paint or Perfect Pearls
- embellishments (brads)
- tacky glue
- sandpaper
- embossing template (American Traditional Designs)
- awl or piercing tool
- craft knife
- brush
- stylus of embossing machine

Instructions

1 Make twelve 4" (10.2 cm) embossed tin squares.

2 Trim the squares so that the embossed image is in the center of a 2¾" (7 cm) square.

This will leave a ½" (1.3 cm) edge around the embossed image.

3 Starting with the center square, adhere the squares on to the vase. Trim the excess edges from the vase with a craft knife.

4 Create a 1¼" × 9" (3.2 × 22.9 cm) hammered metal strip and adhere it to the rim of the vase.

5 Make any adjustments to the coloring and distressing using paint or Perfect Pearls and sandpaper.

6 Use an awl or piercing tool to punch holes around the embossed squares and insert the brads in to the holes.

7 Add patina and aged effects by sanding and stippling with patina colored paints.

It is hard to imagine this gorgeous wall vase is made entirely from paper. Embossed tin and hammered metal techniques are used to create individual squares that are adhered to a papier-mâché base. The result is a custom decorative piece for the home.

Painted Tin Frame

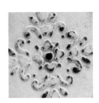

RECIPES AND TECHNIQUES

Painted Tin

MATERIALS

- papier-mâché (Jade Kraft, frame)
- card stock (black)
- embellishments (brads)
- paint
- adhesive
- sandpaper
- embossing template (American Traditional Designs)
- brush
- stylus of embossing machine

Instructions

1 Create a flat painted tin piece and cover the frame.

2 Make four 2" (5.1 cm) painted tin squares with the embossing template.

3 Trim each embossed piece to a 1³⁄₄" (4.4 cm) square.

4 Adhere the squares on to four flat painted tin panels that are each 2" (5.1 cm) square.

5 Attach brads in each corner of the embossed squares and then adhere the four finished pieces to each corner of the frame.

6 Sand the brads and the edges of the frame.

Shabby chic never looked better than this faux-finished frame that mimics the look of weathered wood and embossed painted tin corners. Don't be afraid to use these techniques on larger projects.

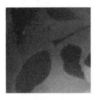

Aged Recipe Sampler

RECIPES AND TECHNIQUES

Direct-to-Paper, Overstenciling, Lifting Color with Bleach, Mottled Paper, Aging Techniques

MATERIALS

- chipboard
- card stock (cream)
- die-cut letters (Cricut, Base Camp)
- dye-based inks
- walnut inks
- bleach laundry pen
- mixing cup
- copies of recipes and artwork

- embellishments (brads, twill tape, staples)
- easel or hanger
- adhesive
- paper towels
- stamps (unknown, alphabet)
- stencil (American Traditional Designs)
- stipple brush or sponge
- spray bottle

Instructions

1 Cover a 6" × 8" (15.2 × 20.3 cm) piece of chipboard with card stock and apply the inks.

2 Using the stencil, sponge or stipple multiple images over the panel with the inks.

3 Squeeze some bleach gel from the laundry pen in to a small mixing cup. Wear gloves and use a sponge to stencil more images (this creates the light-colored stenciled images.)

4 Cut and tear pocket pieces, recipe card frames, and a photo tag from card stock. Apply inks to all the pieces and then mottle them.

5 Add stenciled images to the front pocket panel, recipe card frames, and the photo tag.

6 Adhere the recipes and photo, and then age the edges with ink.

7 Stamp words onto the twill tape and staple to the recipe cards.

8 Assemble the sampler with adhesive and brads.

9 Ink more card stock and mottle it. Cut out the letters for "Recipes" and age the edges with ink.

10 Adhere the letters to the front pocket (use foam tape for dimension).

11 Attach an easel or hanger to the back of the chipboard panel.

This heirloom-looking display showcases family recipes that have been passed down through the generations. Stencils are used to create the effects of stunning vintage wallpaper that is used to cover the piece.

Patina Communicate Portfolio

RECITES AND TECHNIQUES

Wax Paper Batik, Aging Techniques, Mottled Paper, Overstamping, Faux Metal

MATERIALS

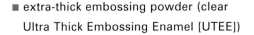

- portfolio (AccuCut, P1494CSJ)
- glossy paper
- card stock (brown, black, cream)
- die cuts (Sizzix, Ransom)
- scrap paper
- dye-based inks
- Perfect Pearls (Patina)
- Perfect Medium
- extra-thick embossing powder (clear Ultra Thick Embossing Enamel [UTEE])

- embellishments (fibers)
- adhesive
- wax paper
- paper towels
- stamps (postal themed)
- felt pressing cloth
- heat tool
- iron
- spray bottle

Instructions

1 Apply the wax paper batik technique to glossy paper and adhere it onto the portfolio's cover.

2 Age the sides and corners of the portfolio and mottle with water.

3 Overstamp images on to the cover.

4 Apply aged and patina effects to die-cut letters. Layer a few of the letters onto card stock that has been inked, mottled, and aged.

5 Adhere letters onto a 3½" × 3⅛" (8.9 × 7.9 cm) piece of card stock that has been inked, mottled, and matted with more of the same card stock. Adhere the entire piece to the portfolio's cover.

6 Layer and adhere several clip die cuts. Stamp an image and apply it to the top of the clip.

7 Apply Perfect Medium over the stamped image. Pour and heat UTEE on top of the image.

8 Use the stamped watercolor effects technique to create a bookmark.

9 Fill the portfolio with items and tie with a string that has been aged.

A handsome portfolio seems well traveled, exhibiting postal-themed stamps from all over the world. The collection inside consists of matching postcards, a paper-wrapped pencil, the look of an intricate watercolor on a bookmark, and a shining tile clip.

RECIPES AND TECHNIQUES

Shining Stones

MATERIALS

- three or four pieces of chipboard (12" [30.5 cm] square)
- three heavy pieces of glossy card stock (12" [30.5 cm] square)
- black card stock
- dye-based inks
- Perfect Pearls (Gold)
- chessmen images
- thirty-two floral marbles
- tacky glue
- clear-drying adhesive or acrylic medium
- ¾" (1.9 cm) and 1½" (3.8 cm) circle punches
- paper towels
- fine-mist spray bottle

Instructions

1 Layer and glue together the chipboard. Clamp them together and let them dry.

2 Make shining stones paper in two colors, using one and a half sheets for each color.

3 Cut the shining stones paper into 1½" x 12" (3.8 x 30.5 cm) strips. For each color, cut the strips into thirty-two 1½" (3.8 cm) squares. Set the leftover strips aside.

4 Draw a line down the center of the chipboard stack to use as a guide when adhering the checkerboard pieces in place. Begin in the center so excess edges can be trimmed from the ends where it will not be as noticeable.

5 Cut out ninety-six 1½" (3.8 cm) circles from the black card stock. Layer and adhere three of the circles together for each of the thirty-two chess pieces.

6 Stamp or print a chessman image small enough to fit under the floral marble and punch them out with the ¾" (1.9 cm) circle punch.

7 Apply clear-drying adhesive or an acrylic medium to the front of each chessman image and glue it to a floral marble.

8 Cut out sixteen 1½" (3.8 cm) circles from each color of the shining stones paper and adhere them to the top of each black card stock stack.

9 Adhere a set of chessmen marbles to the same color discs, then adhere the other set on the other color.

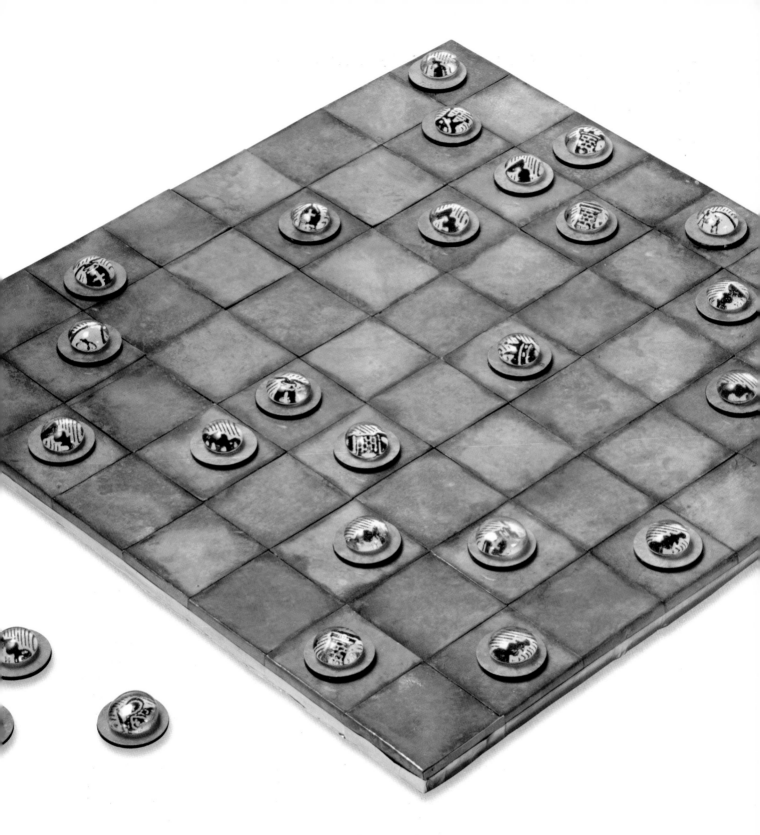

This is a remarkably lightweight version of a heavy traditional stone chess set. Four layers of chipboard are covered in two colors of shining stone paper for the ideal checkerboard base. Shining stone paper is also made into discs to house the images of the chess pieces accented with floral marbles.

RECIPES AND TECHNIQUES

Spackle Paste Paper

MATERIALS

- card stock (teal, cream, black)
- die cut (AccuCut, S21605)
- dye-based inks
- spackling paste
- polymer medium
- embellishments (ribbon, mesh, staples)
- adhesive
- craft knife
- palette knife
- raking tool (fork)
- hole punch
- mirror 5" (12.7 cm) in diameter

Instructions

1 Apply the spackle paste technique to cream card stock. When dry, trim the card stock to 5⅜" (13.7 cm) square.

2 Lightly slide ink over the spackled surface to add color and highlights.

3 Mat the spackled paper piece on cream card stock and ink the edges. Mat again with teal card stock and ink the edges.

4 Cut a 3" (7.6 cm) circle from the center of the layered pieces.

5 Attach the mirror to the back with a strong adhesive.

6 Back the frame with two or three layers of black card stock to make the frame sturdy.

7 Create an easel by attaching a 2" (5.1 cm) strip of heavy black card stock. Make a crease ½" (1.3 cm) from the top and fold outward.

8 Attach a ribbon to the bottom of the easel and the frame to make the easel stronger.

9 Punch a starfish out of the scrap 3" (7.6 cm) center of the spackled paper.

10 Place mesh on the corner of the frame and add the starfish to the top.

11 Attach ribbons to the side of the frame with a hole punch and a stapler.

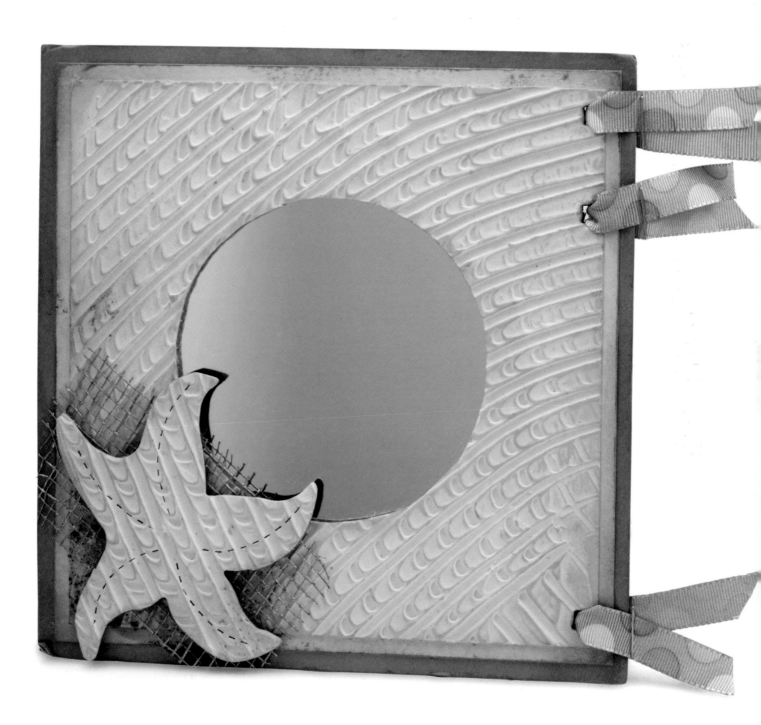

A layer of spackle paste is spread across card stock and transformed into a textural marvel with a fork. A ribbon, mesh, and a textured starfish add to this whimsical sea theme.

RECIPES AND TECHNIQUES

Pearly Mottled Paper, Faux Sea Glass, Shimmer Paper, Shimmer Paper

MATERIALS

- papier-mâché (JuliaAndrus.com, 7" [17.8 cm] square frame)
- card stock (dark green)
- illustration board (white)
- dye-based inks
- Perfect Medium
- Perfect Pearls (Interference Blue, Interference Green, Sunflower Sparkle, Pearl)
- extra-thick embossing powder (clear Ultra Thick Embossing Enamel [UTEE])
- quote or picture
- embellishments (brads, ribbon)
- adhesive
- paper towels
- spray bottle
- brayer
- brush
- heat gun

Instructions

1 Apply the pearly mottled paper technique directly to the frame.

2 Tear the illustration board into two small squares and apply the faux sea glass technique.

3 Apply the shimmer paper technique on a 3" (7.6 cm) square of card stock. When dry, cut the corner piece for the frame and attach the three brads along the top.

4 Tie the ribbon on to the frame, and then adhere the faux sea glass pieces and the gold corner.

5 Insert the quote or picture.

TIP

□ To make a custom-colored ribbon, press a satin ribbon into dye-based ink. Crumple the ribbon in a paper towel and spray with water. Compress the ribbon firmly in the paper towel and unfold. The results will be a beautifully mottled faux-silk ribbon.

The voice of the sea may speak to the soul, but so does the serenity of this frame. A pearly mottled finish is applied to the frame before it is wrapped with ribbon. Faux sea glass and a corner made from shimmer paper add the final touches.

Watercolor Stained Bookmark

RECIPES AND TECHNIQUES

Watercolor Staining

MATERIALS

- watercolor paper
- card stock (purple, orange)
- art board or chipboard
- watercolors
- dye-based ink
- embellishments (eyelet, ribbons)
- artist tape
- adhesive
- pen or marker (black)
- stamp (Hampton Arts, Woman in Coat [DF2296])
- brush
- hole punch

Instructions

1 Following the watercolor staining technique, paint a colored rectangle on a 3" × 6" (7.6 × 15.2 cm) piece of watercolor paper.

2 Stamp the image inside the painted area, and use a pen to write around the rectangle.

3 Mat the image on orange card stock then again on purple card stock.

4 Punch a hole in the corner of the bookmark and attach the eyelet and ribbons.

On the bookmark (calligraphy): But love is such a mystery, I cannot find it out; For to think in best resolved, I then am in most doubt.

Sir John Suckling 1609-1642

A stained background, a stamped image, and a little calligraphy make this bookmark a work of art. Use a fountain pen or a calligraphy nib for more artistic writing.

Embossed Pencil Box

RECIPES AND TECHNIQUES

Painted Tin, Embossed Tin, Dry Embossing

MATERIALS

- papier-mâché (JuliaAndrus.com, long box)
- card stock (black, beige)
- acrylic paint (green)
- Perfect Pearls (Pewter)
- embellishments (brads, ribbon)
- adhesive
- stamp (Hero Arts, Dream & Discover)
- stencil (Paula Hallinan, PRH-443)
- texture plate (Ellison, Diamonds; Fiskars, Braids)
- stylus
- embossing machine
- sandpaper
- brush

Instructions

1 Apply the painted tin technique to black card stock and trim to a 9" × 3½" (22.9 × 8.9 cm) rectangle.

2 Apply the embossed tin technique to black card stock. Trim two pieces to 3½" × 1" (8.9 × 2.5 cm) and adhere to the top and bottom of the painted tin.

3 Stamp the quote onto beige card stock and trim to a 3½" × 1½" (8.9 × 3.8 cm) strip. Ink the edges of the strip and adhere below the embossed tin piece.

4 Dry-emboss the seaull image onto beige card stock. Glide ink over the raised image and along the edges.

5 Attach the dry-embossed image with the brads onto the painted tin. Adhere the entire piece to the top of the papier-mâché box.

6 Tie a ribbon around the box.

TIP

☐ Perfect Pearls were used with water to form a creamy paint for the embossed tin.

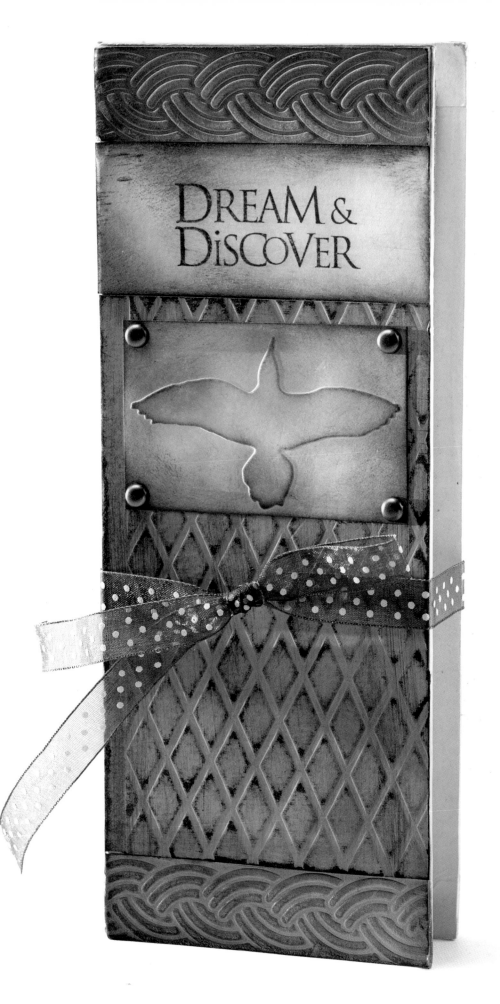

DREAM & DISCOVER

Receive high marks with this class-act pencil box. Faux-painted tin is trimmed with beautiful faux embossed tin and then layered with an aged dry-embossed image.

RECIPES AND TECHNIQUES

Pastel Masking, Filigree

MATERIALS

- card stock (cream, black, brown, teal)
- die cuts (Sizzlits, Architectural Accents #1)
- pastels
- dye-based ink
- paint (gold)
- adhesive
- embellishments (fibers, beads)
- stamp (Stampers Anonymous, K1-646)
- pastel applicator

Instructions

1 Tear a scrap piece of card stock to create a mountain shape. Use the shape as a mask on a 4" (10.2 cm) square piece of cream card stock and apply pastels to create a sky.

2 Remove the mask and apply pastels to the mountain shape.

3 Stamp the quote onto the pastel piece.

4 Create the filigree and adhere to the corner of the pastel piece.

5 Adhere a photo corner out of black card stock opposite the filigree.

6 Mat with black card stock and adhere to a 5" (12.7 cm) square of brown card stock.

7 Adhere the piece to a 5⅝" (14.3 cm) square teal card.

8 Apply pastels to the edges of the card stock.

9 Thread beads over the fiber and tie to the card.

Employing pastel and masking technique creates this dreamscape of a card. The card is complemented with flyaway fibers and beads of the same colors. Ornate faux-metal filigree completes the card.

Mottled Book of Days

RECIPES AND TECHNIQUES

Direct-to-Paper, Mottled Paper, Lifting Color with Bleach, Stamped Watercolor Effects, Aging Techniques, Hardware

MATERIALS

- paper (white; Jade Kraft, Renaissance Rag)
- card stock (teal, rose, black)
- vellum
- die cuts (Sizzix, Ransom; AccuCut, hinge #3 2H1702L)
- dye-based inks
- acrylic paint
- embellishments (brads, ribbon, wax linen)

- adhesive
- bleach pen
- stamps (Limited Edition, JV267D; Stamp Francisco, woman; brand unknown, print wheel)
- sandpaper
- paper towels
- spray bottle

Instructions

1 Create a book by first cutting four 6" × 12" (15.2 × 30.5 cm) rectangles from Renaissance Rag paper and one from vellum. Layer and fold the sheets so one paper is on top followed by the vellum and then the remaining paper. Pierce two holes along the fold and tie the book together with the wax linen.

2 Apply the inks to an 11" × 17" (27.9 x 43.2 cm) sheet of paper and mottle with water. Fold the paper into a book cover and slip it over the book.

▶

3 Stamp, using the bleach, onto the front cover and ink the edges of the cover.

4 Apply the inks to a 6¼" × 3" (15.9 × 7.6 cm) piece of rose card stock, mottle with water, and tear the bottom edge. Ink the edges and adhere to the front cover.

5 Use the stamped water-color effects technique to stamp the image of the woman and an "A" onto paper.

11" × 17" (27.9 × 43.2 cm)

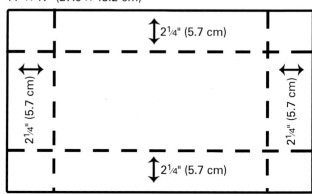

2¼" (5.7 cm)

2¼" (5.7 cm)

2¼" (5.7 cm)

2¼" (5.7 cm)

2¼" (5.7 cm)

Insert over back page of booklet

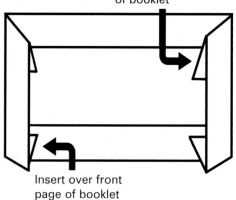

Insert over front page of booklet

6 Trim the image of the woman and mat with both teal and rose card stock. Ink the edges and adhere to the front cover.

7 Ink the edges of the "A" and adhere to the cover, overlapping image of the woman.

8 Stamp the words "book of" on to rose card stock and tear the edges. Ink the edges and adhere to the cover, overlapping the image of the woman.

9 Die-cut the letters "days" and apply ink before adhering to the front cover.

10 Paint, ink, and sand the hardware hinge before attaching to the cover with brads.

11 Tie a ribbon around the book.

Keep track of important annual dates with this colorful masterpiece. Inside is a page for each month with blank lines to record information.

Stamped Violette Card

RECIPES AND TECHNIQUES

Mottled Paper, Aging Techniques, Resist on Glossy, Overstamping, Hammered Copper

MATERIALS

- glossy paper (white)
- card stock (red, white, black)
- die cuts (Paper Shapers, flower; Family Treasures, flower)
- dye-based inks
- Perfect Pearls (Copper)
- Perfect Medium
- embellishments (brads, buttons)
- stamps (Stampers Anonymous, U1-846; Tin Can Mail, 91599.X)
- paper towels
- spray bottle

Instructions

1 Create a 6" × 7" (15.2 × 17.8 cm) card out of red card stock and ink the edges.

2 Apply the inks to white card stock and mottle with water. Tear and ink the edges before adhering the piece to the card.

3 Create a sheet of patterned paper using the resist on glossy technique. Cut out a 4½" × 6" (11.4 × 15.2 cm) rectangle from the paper. Stamp an image onto the paper, ink the edges, and adhere it to the card.

4 Cut out flower shapes from the patterned paper and set aside.

5 Overstamp on the reaming patterned paper and cut out the diamonds. Adhere them along the right side of the card along with the buttons.

6 Layer and adhere 1½" × ½" (3.8 × 1.3 cm) strips of black card stock together and apply a metal finish with Perfect Pearls. Embed the words *dance* and *sing* into the strips and adhere to the card.

7 Make a ¼" × 7" (6 mm × 17.8 cm) strip of hammered copper and adhere to the card.

8 Cut a flower shape from excess mottled paper and layer with the patterned paper flowers. Ink the edges and attach to the card with a brad.

This card displays a bouquet of paper techniques. A strip of faux-hammered metal is adhered and embellished with floral punches. Opposite the strip is a row of over-stamped diamonds decorated with buttons. The card is finished off with embedded word tiles.

Stone Clock in a Box

RECIPES AND TECHNIQUES

Shining Stones, Aging Techniques, Hardware, Hammered Gold

MATERIALS

- card stock (glossy white, black)
- paper (white)
- die cuts (Cricut, Stamped; AccuCut, Photo Holders #1, T11215)
- dye-based inks
- walnut inks
- Perfect Pearls (Gold)
- computer-generated quote and image
- embellishments (ribbon, brads, floral marble)
- clock
- paper towels
- stamps (A Stamp in the Hand Co., script)
- hole punch
- brush
- brayer
- spray bottle

Instructions

1 Apply the shining stones technique on the glossy paper then die-cut and assemble the box.

2 Stamp text onto paper and tear into pieces. Dye strips with walnut inks and adhere them to the box.

3 Make two handles and attach to the box with adhesive and brads.

4 Place the main part of the clock into the box and attach the hands through a hole that has been punched in the lid.

5 Apply the hammered gold technique to black card stock and die-cut the numbers. Adhere the numbers to the clock.

6 Print out "Time is of the Essence" and adhere underneath a floral marble before adhering it to the clock.

7 Create a tag using extra pieces of the matching papers. Mat an image in the hammered gold paper and adhere to the tag.

8 Die-cut several oval tags from black card stock and adhere together. Embed the word "live" in to the tag and apply a gold finish with Perfect Pearls.

9 Tie a ribbon around the box and tie on tags.

This shining stone treatment is done on glossy card stock and folded into a box. The box is decorated with paper strips that have been torn, dyed, and aged. Faux-metal handles are attached to the top with an elegant ribbon strung through them. Matching tags are added as a final step.

Leather Desk Set

RECIPES AND TECHNIQUES

Leather Paper, Painted Tin, Color Lifting, Handles

MATERIALS

- card stock (teal)
- Perfect Pearls (Pewter)
- dye-based ink
- color lifting pad (Jacquard, Castaway Stamp Pad)
- Perfect Ink Refresher
- embellishments (brads, string, charms)
- adhesive
- sandpaper
- texture plate (Ellison, Paisleys)
- embossing machine
- iron

Instructions

1 Make six sheets of leather paper using 12" (30.5 cm) square teal card stock.

2 Glide the color lifting pad and a contrasting dye-based ink over the leather paper and iron the paper flat.

3 Make two sheets of painted tin paper.

4 Lay four of the leather sheets together, creating a 24" (61 cm) square for the desk set base.

5 Cut one of the reaming leather papers into four 3" × 12" (7.6 × 30.5 cm) strips. Adhere one strip over each seam of the desk set base.

6 Cut a 3" (7.6 cm) square from the painted tin paper. Adhere to the center of the desk set base and attach brads in each corner.

7 Cut four triangles out of painted tin paper and adhere to the corners of the desk set base. Attach brads across the long side of the triangles.

8 Use the leather and tin paper to cover a pencil holder, a pen, and a book cover for sticky notes. Tie charms onto the objects using string.

9 Attach a handle to the book cover with brads.

A sophisticated leather desk set is the perfect way to organize a desk. The complete set is a faux-leather base trimmed in painted tin along with a matching pen, pencil holder, and sticky-note pad cover.

RECIPES AND TECHNIQUES

Tortoiseshell, Polished Metals, Extra-thick Embossing

MATERIALS

- metal tin
- glossy paper (white)
- die cuts (AccuCut, 2ZB2503L)
- alcohol inks (Ranger Industries: Pitch Black, Butterscotch, Espresso)
- alcohol blending solution
- spray paint (glossy black)
- Perfect Pearls (Gold)
- Perfect Medium
- extra-thick embossing powder (gold Ultra Thick Embossing Enamel [UTEE])
- embellishments (ribbon)
- adhesive
- stamps (postal themed)
- ink applicator
- heat tool

Instructions

1 Paint the metal tin black and let dry.

2 Apply the tortoiseshell technique to a glossy paper and adhere it to the lid.

3 Create a dimensional token using the extra-thick embossing technique and adhere to the lid.

4 Create a buckle using the polished metal technique and attach it to the tin with ribbon.

Re-create the luxurious look of tortoiseshell with an alcohol ink method. A lacquered glossy black tin hosts the tortoise-shell along with an embedded stamped image.

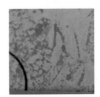

Marbled Travel Shrine

RECIPES AND TECHNIQUES

Luminous Marbling, Shining Stones, Over-stamping

MATERIALS

- papier-mâché (JuliaAndrus.com, folding screen)
- card stock (glossy white, black, orange, red, white)
- die cuts (Ellison, Architectural Accents #2)
- dye-based ink
- Perfect Ink Refresher
- Perfect Pearls (Kiwi, Turquoise, Berry Twist, Gold)
- embellishments (fiber, photo corners)
- keepsakes and photographs
- paper towels
- stamps (postal-themed)
- brush
- brayer
- fine-mist spray bottle

Instructions

1 Create luminous marbled paper and adhere it to the outside of the folding screen.

2 Create shining stones paper and adhere it to the inside of the folding screen. Randomly stamp images over the paper.

3 Tear pieces of the luminous marbled paper to create pockets on the outside panels of the folding screen.

4 Die-cut decorative shapes from the shining stones paper and adhere them over the pockets.

5 Mat some of the photos and keepsakes with orange, red, and white card stock. Tie on fibers.

6 Attach some of the photos and keepsakes to the frame along with die cuts and photo corners. Add the remaining items to the pockets.

Whatever the destination, displaying keepsakes and photos
from a special experience is particularly charming and easy
to share in a shrine. This shrine is covered in a luminous
marbled paper on the outside and a gold veined paper on
the inside.

Faux Alligator Purse Card

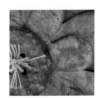

RECIPES AND TECHNIQUES

Dry Embossing, Hammered Metal, Direct-to-Paper, Aging Techniques

MATERIALS

- card stock (green)
- paper (white)
- die cuts (AccuCut, B2501; Sizzix, 38-1135)
- dye-based inks
- glossy acrylic spray
- embellishments (brads, beads, ribbon)
- texture plate (Fiskars, Leather)
- embossing machine
- adhesive

Instructions

1 Spray a thin coat of glossy acrylic over the green card stock and run it through the embossing machine with the texture plate.

2 Die-cut the purse shape from the embossed paper.

3 Create a sheet of hammered metal, and die-cut the purse top and the button from it.

4 Adhere the purse top and attach the brads.

5 Apply inks to the paper and then die-cut flowers from it. Ink the edges of the flowers and attach to the purse along with the hammered metal button.

6 Tie a ribbon to one side of the purse, string with beads, and tie to the other side.

7 Tie ribbon to the sides of the purse.

No alligators were injured for this process! Actually, the alligator paper started as green card stock that is painted with a thin coat of glossy acrylic and then dry-embossed in a personal die-cut/embossing machine.

Mottled Dressed Mannequin

RECIPES AND TECHNIQUES

Mottled Paper, Stamping, Aging Techniques, Heat Embossing

MATERIALS

- papier-mâché (JuliaAndrus.com, mannequin)
  card stock (white)
- tissue paper (white, gold)
- dye-based inks
- watercolors
- paint (gold)
- embossing powder (white)
- embellishments (rivets, pearls, ribbon)
- paper towels
- stamps (Top-Embossing Arts, floral cube)
- rivet setter
- candle holder
- heat tool
- spray bottle

Instructions

1 Paint the mannequin gold and let it dry. Adhere the gold tissue paper to a candle holder and glue the mannequin to it.

2 Spray watercolors onto white tissue paper and let it dry.

3 Heat-emboss a floral design onto the tissue paper and drape it over the top portion of the mannequin.

4 Create three different colors of mottled paper. Mottle both sides of the card stock, alternating the colors.

5 Cut out nine petal shapes from the mottled paper and ink the edges. Stamp words and images on two or three of the petals.

6 Overlap the petals into a semicircle and attach them to each other with rivets.

7 Attach ribbon onto the end petals and tie the skirt onto the mannequin. Curl the ends of the petals up.

8 Cut a strip of mottled paper and adhere it to the mannequin as a belt.

9 Embellish with pearls and a paper corsage made from mottled paper scraps.

Mottled card stock petals are arranged into a full skirt for this papier-mâché mannequin. She is dressed up with some pearls and a paper corsage then glued to a candle holder covered in gold tissue.

Marbled Journal Book

RECIPES AND TECHNIQUES

Marbled Paper, Dry Embossing, Polished Metal

MATERIALS

- blank journal
- paper
- card stock (black)
- die-cut
- marbling supplies
- glossy acrylic spray
- stencil (Lasting Impression, B270)
- embellishments (braids, ribbon)
- stamp
- ink
- adhesive

Instructions

1 Apply a marbling technique to the paper and adhere it to the cover of the journal.

2 Trim black card stock to fit over the binding and paint with the glossy acrylic.

3 Emboss the black strip and adhere it onto the journal.

4 Embellish the journal with embossed corners, contrasting marble paper tags and title, and a polished metal key.

A purchased blank journal is covered in handmade marbled paper. To make the leather bindings appear real, black card stock is painted with glossy acrylic paint and then dry-embossed for added interest. Even the key is paper.

Marbled Pinwheel

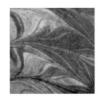

RECIPES AND TECHNIQUES

Marbled Paper

MATERIALS

- paper
- marbling supplies
- embellishments (ribbon)
- wooden dowel
- adhesive
- brad

Instructions

1 Apply a marbling technique to the paper.

2 Cut the marbled paper and fold it into a pinwheel and secure with a brad.

3 Wrap the ribbons around the wooden dowel and adhere the ends.

4 Attach the pinwheel to the wooden dowel.

Beautiful marbled papers are turned into a playful pinwheel
that spins these unique papers around and around.

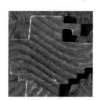

Leather Phoenix Accordion Album

RECIPES AND TECHNIQUES

Leather Paper, Hammered Copper, Luminous Paste

MATERIALS

- accordion album
- card stock (black, rust)
- die cut (AccuCut, CRB800J)
- Perfect Pearls (Patina)
- Perfect Ink Refresher
- Glossy Accents
- embellishments (brads)
- adhesive
- sandpaper
- iron
- brush

Instructions

1 Create leather paper and adhere to the cover of the accordion album.

2 Create a sheet of hammered copper paper. Cut out four triangles from it and adhere them to each corner of the cover.

3 Cut a strip out of the hammered copper paper and adhere it to the lower-right corner. Attach brads along the strip.

4 Create a sheet of luminous paste paper. Die-cut the phoenix shape and adhere it to the cover.

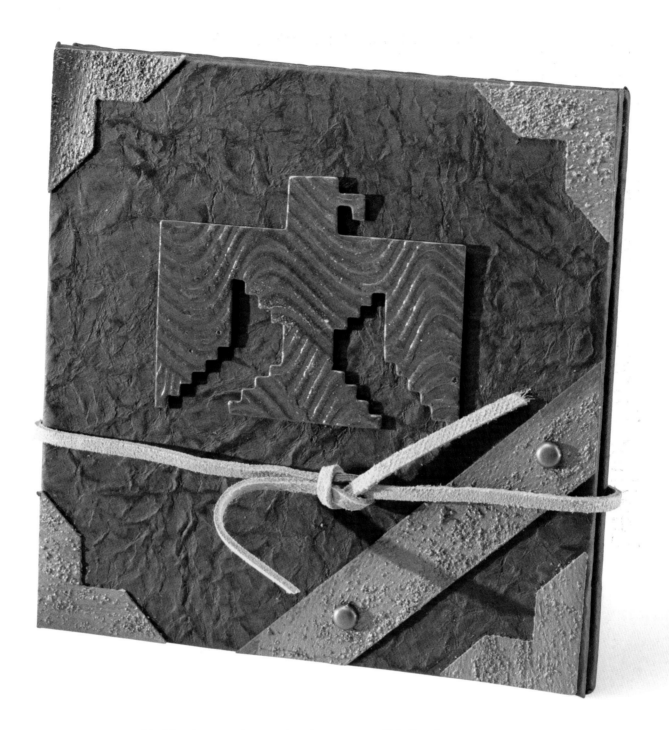

Nothing is more interesting than texture. This Southwestern album begs to be picked up and handled. The front cover is leather paper trimmed with corroded faux-metal corners. Luminous paste paper is used for the phoenix bird.

International Resources

AUSTRALIA

Eckersley's Art & Craft
(store locations in
New South Wales,
Queensland, South
Australia, and Victoria)
www.eckersleys.com.au
art and craft supplies

CANADA

Curry's Art Store
800.268.2969
www.currys.com
Ontario
art and craft supplies

Lazar StudioWERX Inc.
www.lazarstudiowerx.com
British Columbia
rubber stamps and art tools

FRANCE

Graphigro
6e arrondissement
133, Rue de Rennes
Paris
www.graphigro.com
33.01.53.36000
art supplies

NEW ZEALAND

**Littlejohns Art & Graphic
Supplies Ltd.**
170 Victoria Street
Wellington
64.04.385.2099
art and craft supplies

UNITED KINGDOM

Derwent
44.017.687.73626
www.pencils.co.uk
watercolor pencils

T N Lawrence & Son Ltd.
208 Portland Road
Hove, BN3 5QT
44.01273.260260
www.lawrence.co.uk
art supplies

Creative Crafts
11 The Square
Winchester
Hampshire, SO23 9ES
44.01962.856266
www.creativecrafts.co.uk
art and craft supplies

HobbyCraft Group Limited
7 Enterprise Way
Aviation Park
Bournemouth International
Airport
Christchurch
Dorset, BH23 6HG
44.01202.596100
www.hobbycraft.co.uk
art and craft supplies

UNITED STATES

AccuCut
800.288.1670
www.accucut.com
die cuts and accessories

**American Traditional
Designs**
800.448.6656
www.americantraditional.
com
stencils and templates

Julia Andrus
www.juliaandrus.com
*art and craft supplies, die
cuts, Perfect Pearls, Perfect
Medium, Perfect Ink
Refresher, papier-mâché,
rice paper*

Clearsnap
888.448.4862
www.clearsnap.com
*dye-based inks, chalk inks,
and pigment inks*

Clorox
www.clorox.com
bleach pen

Ellison Design
888.598.8808
www.ellisondesign.com
*embossing and die-cut
accessories*

Jacquard
800.442.0455
www.jacquardproducts.com
*marbling kits, Castaway
Stamp Pad, and alcohol inks*

JudiKins
310.515.1115
www.judikins.com
stamps

La D'ore
310.204.2451
www.la-dore.com
metal leafing supplies

Magenta
450.922.5253
www.magentastyle.com
stamps

Prism Paper
866.902.1002
www.prismpapers.com
card stock and papers

Provo Craft
800.937.7686
www.provocraft.com
*craft supplies, stamps, and
Cricut*

Ranger Industries Inc.
732.389.3535
www.rangerink.com
*dye-based inks, compressed
sponge, ink, alcohol ink,
Perfect Pearls, Perfect
Medium, Perfect Ink
Refresher, Ultra Thick
Embossing Enamel (UTEE),
and heat-embossing
products*

Stamp Francisco
360.210.4031
www.stampfrancisco.com
stamps

Stampers Anonymous
800.945.3980
www.stampersanonymous.
com
stamps

**Suze Weinberg Design
Studio**
www.schmoozewithsuze.com
*Ultra Thick Embossing
Enamel (UTEE) and
accessories*

Tsukineko
800.769.6633
www.tsukineko.com
walnut inks

About the Artist

Julia Andrus is an artist, designer, presenter, teacher, and product consultant. She attended art school in Minneapolis with a focus on textile arts, which included illustration and organic chemistry. She worked as a chemist technician for the Honeywell Corporation while in Minneapolis before devoting fifteen years to freelance graphic design and illustration while raising a family.

Julia attended broadcast training in Tampa, Florida, and is an approved presenter with HSN (Home Shopping Network) where she has represented Duncan products as well as her own signature craft product lines. Julia has appeared numerous times on HGTV (Home and Garden Television) and DIY (Do-it-Yourself Network). She continues to write and produce television and media materials that promote the arts.

She has helped develop numerous craft products for leading craft manufacturers and has licensed her name to the Perfect line of products by Ranger Industries, Clear by Design Polymer Stamps by Duncan, and Jade Stamps by Jade Kraft industries. Her art and design work is widely published, and she teaches and demonstrates nationally and internationally.

Acknowledgments

I would be remiss if I did not acknowledge the countless others who have gone before me who have given so liberally and inspired so greatly. The methods in these pages are the results of many contributions and generous acts of sharing. It would be impossible to name them all, so I am forced to extend a universal expression of heartfelt appreciation to all the teachers, artists, crafters, and designers who have contributed to my own knowledge and know-how.

They say inspiration comes from life, so I must mention my twin sister, Jean, who keeps my walls covered in her magnificent art pieces and never ceases to inspire me; Ken, Chris, Ryan, Robyn, Jaime, and Stephanie, who keep me grounded and in touch with the best things in life, including a new generation of little artists; and my husband, who has given me the world to see and thinks it's way cool that *I do art*.

I'd like to thank the manufacturers and television production companies that have promoted me and allowed me to use my talents and creativity to promote the arts and crafting. I have had many great experiences. I must also mention my appreciation to all the students and class participants with whom I have shared countless creative and fun-filled hours.

I work with a great team of individuals. So I offer a warm and special thanks to Stephanie and Cari and the editors at Quarry, who are a delight to work with. Everybody shared the vision enthusiastically and this project was a joy. Thank you everyone who contributed to and supported the process.